Church Street, Boonton. Oil painting by Herbert T. Borgstrom from pencil sketch (1867) erroneously called Brook Street.

Boonton Was An Iron Town

PETER C. WENDT, JR.

Published by
The Boonton Historical Society and Museum

Second Edition

Second Edition
Printed in USA in 1976. Second Edition paperback printed in 2002.
Published by the Boonton Historical Society and Museum
210 Main Street
Boonton, NJ 07005
973-402-8840
www.boonton.org

MISSION STATEMENT: The Boonton Historical Society and Museum is a non-
profit organization incorporated in 1959, located in the town of Boonton, New
Jersey. Its mission is to: 1) preserve and protect the town of Boonton's unique cul-
tural, architectural and industrial history; 2) preserve and share the area's rich history, folklore, arts and humanities of the past and present; 3) encourage preserva-
tion and restoration of historic landmarks in the town; 4) protect and display the
museum's collections; and 5) provide educational programs, guided historical
tours and exhibitions to a diverse population.

Project Coordinator, Production Editor, and
Image Research: Heather Wendt Kemp.
Design and Layout: Cindy Talocci.
Cover Design: Stephen Barth

Photographs:
All photos from the collection of the Boonton Historical Society and
Museum unless otherwise specified. Adjacent to title page, 20: Wendt
Family. 27*t.*, *b.*, 39: Courtesy of the Local History Department, Joint Free
Public Library of Morristown and Morris Township. 28: Courtesy of Ed
Stecewicz, 40*t.*, *b.*: Courtesy of George Eastman House. 47, 117: Courtesy
of the Boonton Holmes Library.

Forward

It's pure and simple, Peter C. Wendt, Jr., loved Boonton.

He was larger than life and with his passion for history, he had the vision to memorialize the early history of our town. It was not because doing so would bring him any fame and certainly not because a book about Boonton would make him wealthy. He did it because, very simply . . . it was a job that needed to be done.

His eldest grandchild, I grew up next door to him and my grandmother Olive Wendt. I had the good fortune to spend my formative years being influenced by his character. Many priceless hours were spent listening to his endless and colorful stories about our town, its history, its citizens and his beloved Boonton Fire Department. As a youngster, I'm afraid that sometimes my eyes would glaze over since I had no idea what he was trying to tell me. Nevertheless, many years later I have grown to appreciate these memories and find myself still surprised by his teachings.

He was a self-educated man, having never finished Boonton High School due to WWI. He was a Master Machinist and a Master Carpenter. He was an accomplished photographer that had an eye for capturing the essence of a scene. A perfectionist, his keen eye for detail was evident in everything that he did. It not only had to look good, it had to feel good to the touch and it wasn't good enough until it did. He was a generous teacher of his craft and could explain things in a way that was easy to grasp by the average person. His talent for writing was self taught and did not come easily to him. We, his family, have all benefited by his guidance in many areas.

He was a very principled and opinionated man. You always knew exactly what he stood for on any issue. He was conflicted in life about the changes that were taking place in America in the 1960's. As a true patriot, it was with pride that he saw his son off to war in WWII, and then went through the same feelings again by sending off his grandson to a questionable American involvement in Vietnam. His emotions were in check that day when I left, but only just barely. During my two combat tours there, his letters to me provided great inspiration and moral support.

The popularity and demand for his book has resulted in this second printing and revalidates his ideas and his efforts to create a published history of Boonton. If he were still with us he would smile his little smile, nod his head in appreciation for this recognition of what to him was a job that had to be done. Then he would go silently back to his work.

Boonton Was An Iron Town is not a book that is read by accident. A person reads this book because they want to learn about the early history of our town or have heard about Boonton from family or friends. Hidden in the history lesson is a portrait of the real character of the citizens of Boonton. It demonstrates the true grit that built Boonton and still remains in the soul of our town today. Built by neighbors, for neighbors, Boonton is a town that by my grandfather's eyes, not only looks right, but feels right.

The Wendt Family sincerely hopes that you all enjoy this book and the efforts of the Boonton Historical Society and Museum. Please support this worthwhile organization and appreciate your heritage and your history. Most of all, be proud of and participate in *your unique community*.

Peter C. Wendt IV
Boonton, New Jersey
USA

The original printer of *Boonton Was an Iron Town* is now out of business and the film from which it was printed is lost. As a result, we have had to recreate the entire book, re-typesetting and researching all of the images. In some cases, the exact photos from the first edition could not be located, so similar shots were substituted. Four photos could not be found in time for this second printing, and substitutes were unavailable, so they were scanned from the first edition. The captions to the substitute photographs have been altered where appropriate, as they may not match my great-grandfather's original. In selecting a font as close to the original style as possible, we found that the pages may break differently. The Table of Contents, and Index reflect the new page numbering. Except for these changes, the text itself has not been altered.
- Heather Wendt Kemp, October 2002.

Second Edition Special Thanks to:
Cindy Talocci, Jeffrey Kemp, Mark Linder, Stephen Barth; The Boonton Historical Society and Museum: Evelyn Eckardt, Edward Marlatt, Eric Wallin, Tammie Holloway; Ed Stecewicz, Ron Rice, Sheri McNeill at the Boonton Holmes Library, the Local History Department of the Joint Free Public Library of Morristown and Morris Township; George Wendt, Elizabeth Masar, Mina Koehler, Peter and Barbara Wendt, Sylvia Lewis.

Preface

With the passing of the centennial years of the Civil War, we were given the opportunity to enlighten ourselves with the many stories written about that great conflict. The majority of these accounts described events in the war itself; only a few related the happenings back home.

While going through some of the references of the war years, and reading of the experiences of the men in this neighborhood, this question presented itself, "What was it like in Boonton and 'Old Pequannoc' a hundred years ago?" The question served as a stimulus in making a more thorough search for information and material pertinent to this area. This quest was found rewarding, not only in the content of the material revealed, but it also brought about the decision to write a history of Boonton.

The original manuscript had been finished to a degree in 1961, and when *The Boonton Years* was being compiled for the Boonton Centennial Committee, access to the manuscript was granted without restriction.

Although the effort was concentrated on the history of the present Boonton, it was decided to include in this work a section of the history of Old Boonton. My good friend, Alex. D. Fowler, had prepared a paper on that subject (published in part in *The Boonton Years, 1867-1967*), and kindly consented to the reproduction of a good part of it here (Chapter I). For that I am very grateful.

By including an historical sketch of Old Boonton, a purpose will be served in that it answers the age old question, "When was Old Boonton 'moved up' to present Boonton?" There were no connections with present Boonton, industrially or otherwise. Incidents happened and individuals lived and labored there, but not in the magnitude depicted and romanticized in stories which the informed consider mostly legend and, quite often, misconception. Nevertheless, an attempt is made to separate the grain from the chaff and to put the gleanings in proper perspective, hoping that history will be served.

The author wishes to express his sincere thanks to Metchie J. E. Budka for his permission to use the descriptive and corroborative information on Old Boonton found in *Under Their Vine and Fig Tree* by Julian Ursyn Niemcewicz, translated and edited by Metchie J. E. Budka, 1965. Published as Vol. XIV in the Collections of the New Jersey Historical Society at Newark.

The Boonton Ironworks rose to national prominence during the Civil War years and detailed accounts were found in a number of textbooks and publications of that era. Nothing was found to support the conjecture that cannon or cannon balls were made in either Old Boonton or in the Boonton Ironworks. The one exception to this was a small cannon made in the Boonton Ironworks in 1860, and a description of this cannon can be found in the text.

An interesting sidelight to the restoration of Boonton's Little Cannon will be found in the appendix. This fine example of research was pursued and brought to completion by Harold W. Schroeder. His knowledge and contacts in the field of metallurgy proved a valuable aid in deciding the point in question. Mr. Schroeder's contribution to this writing is sincerely acknowledged.

The search for documentary evidence in regard to several facets of Boonton's history led to the library at Rutgers University. Donald A. Sinclair, Curator of Special Collections at Rutgers, brought to my attention and had copies made for my use two revealing sources of Boonton's history. The first, "Right and Wrong in Boonton, No. 1," printed by Dr. John Crimes in 1840, relates to the problems of the abolitionists in Boonton. The other, "A History of Schools in Morris County, N.J.," 1876, is a manuscript in which the Boonton portion was written by the Hon. John L. Kanouse. My sincere thanks to Donald A. Sinclair and his staff for making these documents available to me.

Barbara Lang, formerly librarian of the Little Falls Library, discovered that several old prints of the Boonton Ironworks were in the collections at Eastman House in Rochester, N.Y. Beaumont Newhall, Director of Eastman House, kindly furnished prints made from the original paper negatives of Victor Provost, 1856, and gave permission to reproduce them in this history. To Barbara Lang and Beaumont Newhall I wish to extend my sincere thanks for their interest and cooperation.

I am greatly indebted to Louise Borgstrom for typing the manuscript, and to Pearl Clark, Evelyn Eckardt and Laura Lee Linder for their helpful suggestions in the preparation of the final draft. I am also grateful to Miriam Conn, Helen Dunn, Edward Hopkins, Barbara Kalata, Gladys Kingsley, Ernest Krauss, Jean Lee, Edward Lenik, Theodore Merkt, Eleanor Mason and James Norman, all having helped in their own way.

Peter C. Wendt, Jr.
Boonton, New Jersey
August, 1975

To my wife Olive
our children
our grandchildren
our great grandchildren

CONTENTS

Chapter I

Old Boonton
1747–1902

In crossing the Washington Street bridge that joins
Boonton with Parsippany-Troy Hills Township (formerly
Hanover Township) one can stop near the far end and look
out across the Jersey City reservoir. There one's thoughts
might turn to Old Boonton, for in the valley, now covered
since 1903 by a great depth of water, and a thousand feet or
so directly out from the bridge to the southeast, lies the center
of the site known as Old Boonton, founded about 225 years ago.

Distinguished for its ironworks of forges, rolling and slitting
mill, Old Boonton owed its existence primarily to the water-
power facilities afforded by the Rockaway River at that point.
At the site chosen for Old Boonton, the fall of the cascading
river and the steeply sloping banks were deemed ideal for the
erection of small power dams. At one time there were at least
three such dams, not very far apart, furnishing power to the
water wheels, which operated the bellows and trip hammers
of the forges and gave motive power to the rolling and slitting
mill as well as to a gristmill and a sawmill.

Equally important to the site was the availability of raw
materials required for producing wrought iron. Not too far
away were the mines of Hibernia and Mount Hope where
iron ore could be obtained. The surrounding dense forests
could furnish the wood for making the enormous quantities
of charcoal that would be required for the forges; and nearby
outcroppings of limestone could supply any needed flux for
the refining process.

Easy access to markets for iron products was also important,
but in that respect the site of Old Boonton was not ideal.
There was, of course, a limited demand for merchant and bar
iron by local farmers, all of whom had blacksmith shops
where they made their own nails and other hardware items

1

used on the farm. The big markets, however, were the cities of Newark and New York. To reach them it was necessary to transport the iron first by pack-horse and later, when roads were improved, by wagon. Although inconveniently removed by some 25 miles from her principal markets, Old Boonton had a slight advantage over the forges located in the more remote hills in the northwest part of the country.

Old Boonton had only a modest claim to fame. Contrary to Isaac S. Lyon's ardent speculations in his *Historical Discourse on Boonton* (Newark, 1873), the ironworks at Old Boonton was not the first in the 13 colonies, nor was it the first in New Jersey, nor, for that matter, even the first in Morris County. Its principal claim to being historically first rests on having been the first in Morris County to have a rolling and slitting mill, which was erected in 1770. The ironworks at Saugus, Massachusetts, complete with forges and slitting mill, had been in operation more than a century earlier;[1] a rolling and slitting mill in Bethlehem Township, Hunterdon County, New Jersey, antedated the one at Old Boonton by 20 years.[2]

Within its limited capacities, Old Boonton furnished a fair quantity of supplies to the patriot forces during the Revolutionary War. There are records showing that Old Boonton furnished axes, iron rods, sheet iron, iron tires, a number of iron cups, 6,000 pairs of horseshoes, 1,800 kettles and 20,000 flints, the last obtained from Boston.[3] The more substantial "sinews of war" such as cannon and cannon balls, were furnished, in this area, by Hibernia and Mount Hope, where large furnaces and casting facilities were then operating.[4] The possibility of Old Boonton furnishing some three-pounder cannon was considered at one time, but there is no record that any were actually supplied.[5] Although Old Boonton contributed but little of the more glamorous munitions to the war effort, it did contribute substantially to vital needs of Washington's army.

The First Ironworks

When Old Boonton was first settled, or when the ironworks was first established we do not know with certainty. We can be fairly certain that there was neither settler nor ironworks in the Boonton area as early as 1715. In the spring of that year a party of surveyors for the Proprietors of West New Jersey came into this area, laid out a number of lots, and made note of what they saw. John Reading, Jr., chief of the party, kept a diary in which he mentions the few settlers they encountered: two or three in Whippany area, one in Montville, and one in Pompton. There was no mention of any settler in the Boonton area, which he described as a wilderness, and no mention of any ironworks anywhere. None of the Proprietors who had accompanied the survey party would accept the tract which contained the site of Old Boonton.[6]

The earliest notice, discovered to date, of an ironworks at Old Boonton is contained in the records of James Alexander for the year 1747–8. He was Surveyor General of the Proprietors of East New Jersey, which group had come into the possession of all the unsold parcels of land in Morris County after 1742. That notice mentioned the ironworks on the Rockaway River, in Morris County, operated by Obadiah Baldwin.[7] Subsequent references to the ironworks confirm that Obadiah Baldwin was the ironmaster at that time. We conclude that Obadiah Baldwin was probably the first ironmaster at Old Boonton.

Obadiah Baldwin

The known facts about the life of Obadiah Baldwin are few. He was the son of John Baldwin of Newark, and had brothers, Josiah, David and John; by 1741 he was a resident of Parsippany (then Hanover Township), but was required in Newark to give bond, with his brothers, for the care of their aged father as late as 1743.[8] Obadiah and his wife, Susannah, were the parents of a son, Martin, who died at the age of three, and was buried in the graveyard at Whippany in 1742.[9] He continued to live in the Parsippany area the rest of his life, being a member of the Presbyterian Church in 1773,[10] and dying by 1797, leaving two sons and a daughter.[11]

In the year 1759, David Ogden of Newark purchased a narrow strip of land containing 23.19 acres embracing both banks of the Rockaway River along most of its course through the present Town of Boonton.[12] The beginning point of the survey of that tract was said to be about one mile above Obadiah Baldwin's ironworks. From the details given in the survey and a map of the river, it is not difficult to show that Obadiah Baldwin's ironworks was at Old Boonton, and that it stood on property already in the possession of David Ogden and William Kelly.

When a county road was laid out in that area in 1761, the ironworks was called "Mr. Ogden's refinery," and the name of Obadiah Baldwin no longer appears in that enterprise.[13] Presumably Obadiah operated the ironworks from the beginning (1747–8) either on lease from Ogden and Kelly, or in their employ, and probably continued his relationship with Ogden until 1765–6, when the management of the works was taken over by Ogden's son, Samuel. We presume that Kelly sold his share to Ogden about 1760, for there is no further mention of his interest.[14]

David Ogden

It was probably in the year 1761 that the village acquired its name of Boone-Town. David Ogden, eminent lawyer of Newark, and for some years a prominent member of the Provincial Council, had but recently become owner of the refinery when Thomas Boone, the new Royal Governor of the province, arrived in July, 1760. Those circumstances support the Ogden-family tradition that the village was named in honor of the new Governor; and the Governor's transfer to

South Carolina in the fall of 1761 makes that year the plausible one for the name to have been given.[15] Neither the name, Boone-Town, nor any of its variants (Boon-town, Boonetown, Booneton or Boonton) has, so far, been found in writings made prior to 1771, in which year Samuel Ogden wrote it, "Boon-Town,"[16] but soon after settled upon "Booneton."[17]

In 1765, David Ogden bought a large tract of land adjacent to his holdings along the Rockaway River in Old Boonton.[18] That tract of 3,656 acres, together with his other lands and those later acquired by Samuel,[19] amounted to more than 4,000 acres. Known as the Great Boonton Tract, it included substantial parts of what are now Mountain Lakes, Town of Boonton, Boonton Township and Taylortown. Apart from being a venture in real estate, the purchase of so large a tract made available ample forests required for making charcoal.

Samuel Ogden

The year 1765 also marked the date of Samuel Ogden's graduation from King's College (now Columbia University). There is a family tradition that Samuel was not in very robust health, and that his doctor had recommended a sojourn in the country. Perhaps it was for that reason that David Ogden induced his 20-year-old son to become resident manager of the ironworks and the Boonton properties.

No description has been found of the ironworks existing in the time of Obadiah Baldwin or at the time when Samuel Ogden took charge. From later descriptions of additions and enlargements of the works, we infer that the early installations were probably limited to one or two forge fires and one or two trip hammers—all on the Hanover side of the river. However small the setup may have been, young Samuel must have seen its possibilities and his vocation. With youthful zeal and energy, Samuel Ogden pursued his plans for expanding the operations at Boone-Town, and for establishing himself as one of the important persons in the community. In 1770 he purchased the Boonton tract from his father,[20] and in August of that year he bought of Thomas Peer a six-acre tract on the opposite bank of the river where he erected a rolling and slitting mill.[21] The machinery for the new mill was purchased in England and at least two experts, Thomas Compson and Thomas Davies, both also from England, were recruited to erect and operate it.[22] The new mill required not only a building to house it, but also wood-burning forge fires for reheating the iron prior to rolling and slitting, as well as a new dam, flume and waterwheel to furnish the necessary power. Part of the capital for this venture was furnished by Samuel's brother, Isaac, and his brother-in-law, Nicholas Hoffman, who were given a 1/6th and 1/8th interest in the mill, respectively.

The expansion of the operations at Old Boonton is reflected in an advertisement that appeared in the *New-York Gazette and Weekly Mercury* on December 28, 1772, and again on April 19, 1773:

SAMUEL OGDEN

Manufactures in the best manner, at his works in Boonetown: bar iron for rudders, grist-mills and sawmills; share moulds, large and small; square and flat iron of all sizes; and also cart, waggon and chair tire: Which he will deliver at New-York on the most reasonable terms, drawn agreeable to any directions, immediately after application made there or, to him at said works, or to Mr. Nicholas Hoffman, merchant, in New York.

The absence of nails from the above list of products can probably be charged to the failure to obtain a "nailer" for whom Samuel had advertised in July, 1771.[23] By 1775, however, at least the smaller nails for shingles and clapboards were being made,[24] and by 1781 card tacks and saddlers tacks, as well as eight sizes of nails were being offered for sale.[25]

The operation of rolling and slitting mills in the American colonies was specifically forbidden by Parliament in 1749–50.[26] The illegality of the mill at Boonetown must have been clearly recognized and condoned by David Ogden, member of the Council and, in 1772, one of the Justices of the Supreme Court.[27] Perhaps the 20-year law had lost some of its force in the atmosphere of rebellion that already was brewing. At any rate the slitting mill was built despite the law, but not without the precaution—so we learn from persistent tradition—of concealing it underneath the gristmill. The mill building is said to have been constructed on a fairly steep bank of the river, and to have had two floors. The main entrance to the mill was on the upper floor, which contained the gristmill; the lower basement floor housed the rolling and slitting mill, and could be entered only from the lower level near the river. However improbable the success of concealing the mill and its reheating furnaces seems to us now, the ruse is alleged to have been successful enough to pass the casual inspection of the well-wined-and-dined Royal Governor, William Franklin.

As manager-owner of a growing ironworks, Samuel found that he had various civic and social responsibilities, which he readily accepted. In 1770, at the age of 24, he was appointed a Justice of the Peace.[28] While serving in that capacity he was instrumental in securing evidence against the notorious counterfeiters headed by Samuel Ford, and received the commendation of the Provincial Council. In the minutes of the Council in 1773 he was referred to as Lieutenant Colonel Samuel Ogden of Morris County, but no notice of his appointment can be found.[29] This may have been an honorary title, but it probably had some semi-official standing because of his organizing his employees and others into a local militia. In 1774, when the colonies began to organize their resistance to the British policy of "taxation without representation," Samuel was named to the county's first Committee of Correspondence, which met at Morristown.[30] The following February he married Euphemia, daughter of Col. Lewis

Morris, and sister of Gouverneur Morris, who was later to distinguish himself in public service.[31] Presumably, Samuel had already built his manor house, which in grandeur may have rivalled Beverwyck in nearby Troy Hills.[32]

Revolutionary War Period

Prior to 1776 most prominent men in New Jersey, as in other colonies, joined Committees of Correspondence and Associations to protest the discriminatory taxes imposed by England. They protested as citizens loyal to the crown, and begged only to be treated as such. When independence was declared, many were shocked, saw only chaos in rebellion and rejected the tenets of the Declaration. Among those so affected were the Ogdens, of whom five of Samuel's kinsmen openly affirmed loyalty to the crown and later joined the Loyalists in New York and Staten Island. They were his father, David, three brothers, Isaac, Nicholas and Peter, and brother-in-law, Nicholas Hoffman.[33] What Samuel's private sentiments were, or those of his brother Abraham, a distinguished lawyer of Morristown, we shall probably never know. Outwardly they supported the Patriot cause.

A number of people—and George Washington himself was one—thought the split loyalties of the Ogden family were designed to save the family fortunes regardless of the outcome of the war. Subsequent events seemed to support that conjecture. When the properties of the defecting Ogdens were seized by the government of New Jersey and sold at auction, Abraham and Samuel were the highest bidders; Abraham bought in his father's property and Samuel that of Isaac Ogden and Nicholas Hoffman.[34] The loyalties of both Abraham and Samuel had already been questioned by the Committee of Safety, and each had taken the oath of allegiance to the Patriot cause.[35] The oath-taking did not absolve them, especially Samuel, from further suspicion of Loyalist sympathies.

In February, 1777, General John Sullivan in Chatham wrote an ominous letter to George Washington warning him to stay away from the vicinity of Samuel Ogden, where Tory sympathy ran high, and where Washington's life might be in danger; the Ogden (presumably Abraham) with whom Washington was then staying was believed to be sincere—but Samuel, No![36] At about the same time, General William Maxwell also wrote Washington complaining of the difficulty of obtaining recruits in this area because of Samuel Ogden's influence in getting deferment for any man who had the slightest disinclination to fight.[37] The Committee of Safety was suspicious of Samuel's motives in buying up the forfeited shares of his kinsmen, and ordered the Attorney General to file a Bill in Equity to discover the true owners and the net profits of the slitting mill.[38] There were also vague charges of Tory activity leveled at Samuel, but, as far as is known, none was ever proved.[39]

Near the end of the war, when the fortunes of the American cause were well advanced, Samuel made an abortive attempt to gain Washington's permission for Isaac Ogden's repatriation. In a letter of reply, Washington aired his suspicions of the motives of the repentant defector, and with scathing rebuke, said he wished to hear nothing more on that subject.[40]

Despite what he claimed were unjust and cruel persecutions by his detractors, Samuel maintained throughout the war the aspect of a true patriot, and placed the resources of the mill at the disposal of the military.[41] The military, in turn, accepted his offer at face value and insistently ordered the various supplies mentioned earlier. In addition, the works at Old Boonton was put on a quasi-military footing—as was done for other ironworks in northern New Jersey—allowing the workers to bear arms in defense of the works, and exempting men from field service except in cases of dire emergency.[42] In his capacity as head of his armed employees, Samuel saw his only military service, if such it could be called. There is no record of any other military service that he performed, although he has erroneously been credited at times with the service record of another Col. Samuel Ogden of Fairfield, Cumberland County, who had eight years of active duty.[43]

Manor house at Old Boonton.

Tax Ratables of 1778

A list of the tax ratables for the year 1778 gives an interesting and probably conservative view of Samuel Ogden's holdings in Old Boonton. North of the Rockaway River, in what was then Pequannock Township, Samuel had one acre of improved land valued at £1,500 (probably the slitting mill lot), and by Fitzpatrick & Hammond. 1,000 acres of unimproved land worth £300. South of the river, in what was then Hanover Township, where his manor house, forge and other village buildings stood, he owned 1,800 acres of improved land worth £7,400, 16 horses, 26 cattle and 6 hogs, all worth £72, and also three slaves, one merchant [shop], two riding chairs or sulkies. He was further listed as having £2,000 lent out at interest. His total rating of about £12,000 shows him to have been one of the wealthiest men in the county.[44]

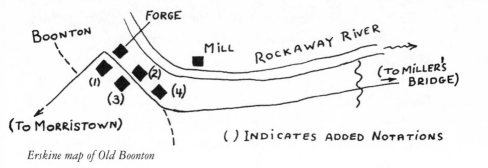

Erskine map of Old Boonton

Military Maps of Old Boonton

During the Revolutionary War there was considerable military traffic over the more or less parallel roads between Morristown and Pompton Plains on the route to the Ramapos and West Point. One of those roads ran from Morristown, through Morris Plains, and on to Old Boonton, following what is substantially the present U.S. Route 202. Near the village the road descended a fairly steep slope almost to the river, where it then made an abrupt turn to the right, passed through the village and followed, in general, the downstream course of the river to Miller's bridge, where Greenbank Road now joins the lower part of Vreeland Avenue; following Vreeland Avenue and River Road, to Montville, it rejoined Route 202 to Lincoln Park, and thence to Pompton Plains. It was along that road that Washington routed the artillery and baggage wagons because Miller's bridge was strong enough to carry the heavy loads.[45] A military map of that road, prepared by Robert Erskine in 1779, shows the village of "Boonton," and indicates the presence of only six buildings, of which only two bear designations: a "forge" between the village road and the right bank of the river, and a "mill" on the left bank.[46]

Erskine's minuscule map of Old Boonton is frustratingly small—about ¼ inch long on the original map—and gives only the barest indication of the size and arrangement of the village. It is, however, the earliest known map of the village and, for that reason, it has been redrawn to a larger scale and reproduced above.

11

Erskine, who made over 200 road maps for Washington, was not the only maker of maps in this region. Thomas Millidge, of Whippany, was a distinguished surveyor of northern New Jersey who turned Tory and joined the Loyalist forces in 1776. From his field notes he prepared a large map of northern New Jersey and southern New York for the use of Loyalist officers. At least two hand-drawn copies of this map, both linen-backed folding maps, exist: one in the Library of Congress, and one (manuscript Map No. 8) in the New York Historical Society. Both maps were drawn about 1780, and differ only slightly in some details. Map No. 8 shows "Boon Town" with six buildings with no designations, but otherwise differs very little from Erskine's map. Still another British map drawn in 1780, the original of which is in the Clements Library at Ann Arbor, Michigan, shows "Boontown," but with less accuracy and detail than the others.

Contemporary deeds, road surveys, and other later information yield a few more clues about the layout of the village and the identity of some of the other buildings shown on the Erskine map. The building we have marked (1) is almost certainly Samuel Ogden's manor house,[47] which surely must have had near it various barns, stables, slave quarters and other dependencies of too little interest to be shown by Erskine. Crossing the river, just below the forge, was a footbridge giving access to the slitting mill lot.[48] The building marked (2) was probably the residence of Nicholas Stagg, who owned a small tract adjoining Ogden's for some time prior to 1773.[49] The building marked (3) has not been identified but it may have been quarters for some of Ogden's employees. Also unidentified is the building marked (4), but it seems to be the same as one indicated on a map of 1853 as "Mrs. Miller" residence. A short distance downstream of the mill was a wagon bridge for crossing the river from the road through the village to the slitting mill lot. The wagon road over that bridge probably continued up the sloping mill lot to the upper level of the mill building to service the gristmill. In 1786 the wagon road was incorporated in a county road, and extended up the hill to include what is now Old Boonton Road.[50] In later years the old bridge was abandoned, and the new one was built about where the old footbridge was.[51] The latter crossing remained in use until the Washington Street bridge was built in about 1900.

Some of the men employed at the mill and forge did not live in the village. Thomas Compson and Thomas Davies, for example, lived about a mile away on the road to Morristown on the lands they had bought from Ogden.[52]

One building of interest, not indicated by Erskine, was the church that Samuel Ogden erected in Old Boonton, probably in the year 1774, or 1775.[53] It was an Anglican Church, and in line with Samuel's professed patriotism, it would have been disbanded by the time the map was made. It may also have been too far away from the road to qualify it as a landmark for Erskine's purposes. Frances Willis (later Mrs. B. F. Howell) recalls that "it stood on the hill above the little brook that crosses the road near the old Miller house . . . ".[54]

The Miller house is doubtless the one we have marked (4), and shown as that of Mrs. Miller on the 1853 map, which also shows the nearby brook.[55] After the Revolutionary War the building was used periodically and alternately by the Reformed Dutch and Protestant Episcopal congregations, as their records show.[56] In 1818 the building was dismantled and used in construction of the Reformed Dutch Church of Montville on a site across the road from the present church building.[57]

Samuel Ogden leaves Old Boonton

From their marriage in 1775, Samuel Ogden and his wife, Euphemia, continued to live at Old Boonton for the ensuing eight years. During that time at least one son, David Bayard Ogden (not David *Boonton* Ogden, as Isaac S. Lyon avers) was born to them. Seven other children were to survive their father, as did David B. Ogden.[58]

13

The war came to a close in 1783, and the British forces withdrew from New York City, which they had occupied for seven years. Tory sympathizers who had taken refuge in the City were evacuated to Canada, Nova Scotia and England. On the heels of the Tory evacuees swept the patriots, who themselves had had to flee the City in 1776. Into the rush, to fill the City's commercial void plunged Samuel Ogden, who opened up a large general store and established his residence in the City in 1783.[59] Perhaps he and his family were not reluctant to leave the area where they bad been the subjects of so much distrust. The management of the ironworks at Old Boonton was placed in the hands of John Jacob Faesch of Mount Hope.

John Jacob Faesch

Born in Basel, Switzerland, in 1729, John Jacob Faesch had already received favorable notice as an ironmaster in Germany, when in 1764 he was offered an attractive contract to come to North America and work with Peter Hasenclever at the ironworks at Ringwood, N.J.[60] Shortly before Faesch and his wife, Johanetta Elizabeth Hegman, were to have embarked for America, his wife died, and he had to make the voyage as a bereaved widower.[61] Upon joining Hasenclever in the ever-expanding operations at Ringwood and vicinity, Faesch served as ironmaster successively at Ringwood, Charlottenburg (later called Charlotteburg) and Long Pond, and became a citizen of New Jersey in 1766.[62] In 1772, after Hasenclever was supplanted as general manager, and Robert Erskine had taken charge, Faesch became dissatisfied, quit his job (his seven-year contract had already expired) and, by lease and purchase, acquired the ironworks and mines on a 6,000-acre tract at Mount Hope, New Jersey.[63]

At Mount Hope, Faesch pursued the business of mining and manufacturing iron with great vigor and skill, and there erected a large furnace in 1772.[64] Three years later, at the age of 46, Faesch married 23-year-old Elizabeth Brinkerhoff and settled in his home, which still stands, in Mount Hope. There two sons and two daughters were born in the succeeding nine years.[65] During the Revolutionary War Faesch furnished substantial quantities of cannon, cannon balls, shells and a variety of cast and hollow-ware products for the Continental Army, and established himself as the foremost ironmaster in New Jersey.[66] After the war he leased and took on the management of other ironworks, including that of Old Boonton, and moved his family to Morristown, where he resided until the death of his wife in 1788.[67]

On April 22, 1788, John Jacob Faesch moved to Old Boonton, residing in the manor house built by Samuel Ogden.[68] Two years later, when Faesch was 61 years old, he married 31-year-old Susanna Leonard, widow of Robed Lawrence, and niece of Captain Michael Kearny of Whippany. Upon her marriage the new Mrs. Faesch became the step-mother of John Jacob, Jr., age 13; Richard Brinkerhoff, age 11; Eliza Maria, age 10; and Catherine Esther, age 5.[69]

The arrangements between Samuel Ogden and Faesch were contained in a lease, dated March 1, 1784, whereby a half interest in the Boonton properties was leased to Faesch for 21 years at an annual rental of £50, with the understanding that they would jointly erect "a four-fire forge and forge hammers with a trip hammer at the place where the old forge, which is now pulled down, at Boonton aforesaid, formerly stood." [70]

That the above improvements and more were carried out, we learn from the journals of two foreign visitors; Theophile Casenove,[71] a representative of the Holland Land Company, who visited Faesch in 1794, and Julian Ursyn Niemcewicz,[72] friend and traveling companion of Kosciuszko, who made visits in 1797 and 1799. Both visitors noted the size of the works which, by 1797, had as many as six forge fires and as many hammers. They also remarked on the novel use of large boiler-like cylinders with pistons that replaced old-fashioned bellows. Niemcewicz noted that Boonton was a very busy place with about 30 employees, mostly German, and was impressed by the din created by crashing waters, turning wheels and pounding hammers. Both remarked on the rustic and wild setting of the village, nestling between steep river banks covered with dense forests; Niemcewicz thought it a very romantic spot. Casenove noted that a half mile away was a church where they preached in Dutch every two weeks.

Further evidence on the extent of the works during the Faesch regime was given by Thomas C. Willis (1791–1864), who as a boy and young man had lived in Old Boonton. In a memorandum written in 1859 for Isaac S. Lyon, he stated that "In 1795 there was a rolling mill and a saw mill, standing in the woods on the east bank of the Rockaway River. On the west bank of the river was a large potash factory, a nail cutting mill, a grist mill and a blacksmith shop. A large building, containing eight refining furnaces, stood where the forge now stands. The pig iron, made at the Mt. Hope and Hibernia blast furnaces, was brought here, refined, rolled and slit into nail rods. There were no less than three dams across the river in the neighborhood of Old Boonton at this time." [73]

John Jacob Faesch* continued the operation of the Boonton works until his death in 1799, after which the management was taken over by his two sons, both in their early twenties.[74] In 1805, when the 21-year lease had run its course, the Faesch brothers purchased the Boonton properties of which, because of previous sales by Ogden, only 2,500 acres remained.[75] Under their management the Boonton works did not prosper—possibly because of their inexperience and a declining market, but also because they were distracted by the pressure of creditors who had resorted to litigation over the Mount Hope properties. In the midst of their financial troubles, John Jacob, Jr., died in 1809 at the age of 33, and Richard B. carried on the works until his death, at 42, in 1820, at which time he was insolvent.[76]

---

* In 1928 a descendant of Faesch generously presented to the Town of Boonton various pieces of jewelry and silver as well as miscellaneous personal effects from the Faesch and Robinson families. A few pieces are on exhibit at Town Hall, where the main part of the collection is in storage.

Neither of the Faesch brothers had married, and their estate (and debts) descended to their sisters, Eliza M., who had married William H. Robinson of New York City in 1801, and Catherine E., who remained unmarried.[77] The heirs sold several lots out of the Boonton tract in the amount of 528 acres in an attempt to prevent foreclosure of the mortgage. On August 18, 1821, the sheriff sold the remaining 1,912 acres of the tract to Israel Crane and William Scott for $8,050.[78]

Israel Crane and William Scott

Israel Crane of Bloomfield and William Scott of Powerville made determined but futile efforts to revitalize the deteriorating ironworks at Old Boonton. At a cost of $20,000 a new and larger dam was built to replace one that had been washed out by a freshet.[79] Dams at Old Boonton were subject to fairly frequent washouts when spring floods, gathered in the 120-square-mile drainage area of the Rockaway River, were funneled through the narrow confines of the river at that point. The new dam was no exception and suffered serious damage shortly after it was built. William Scott himself moved to Old Boonton in 1823, occupied the Ogden Faesch mansion and supervised repairs and new construction, which were going on at great expense.[80] Unhappy with the way things were going at Old Boonton, Crane sold his half interest to Scott on August 28, 1824, for $2,000.[81] Shortly afterward, Scott returned to Powerville where he built his mansion house—now the Sarah Frances Nursing Home—about the year 1825–6.[82]

Scott's leaving Old Boonton and building his new home in Powerville may have been occasioned by his marriage to his second wife, Susannah Munn (his first wife, Susan Dodd, had died in 1822), but more likely by the intelligence he had received concerning the newly proposed Morris Canal.[83] By 1824, the surveyors for the canal had decided to route the canal via Powerville and through Scott's property that

17

extended down the river to a point below the Boonton falls; from that point the canal was to veer eastward to Montville, completely bypassing Old Boonton.[84]

Old Boonton's Last Years

Never again was Old Boonton to flourish as it had in the days of the senior John Jacob Faesch. Its pride, the old slitting mill, had long since been in ruins, and its dams and waterwheels needed extensive repairs; most of the workers had drifted away, and even the church had been torn down and removed to Montville.[85]

We do not know for certain whom William Scott left in charge of the works when he moved away from Old Boonton in or about 1825. It may have been Thomas C. Willis, who is known to have lived in the Ogden-Faesch mansion as late as 1834.[86] At any rate, William Scott continued to own the property until 1836, when he sold two lots, one of 165 acres and one of five acres, comprising the Old Boonton Tract, to his son, Elijah D. Scott.[87] One writer states that John Righter operated a forge and gristmill at Old Boonton for many years following the dissolution of the Crane-Scott partnership.[88] If so, it must have been under an arrangement with the Scotts, for ownership of the property did not come into the hands of the Righter family until 1841, when Samuel F. Righter and Charles A. Righter purchased it from Elijah D. Scott.[89] Neither the small-scale operations carried on by Willis and the Righters, nor the establishment of the Morris County Poor Farm nearby in 1837–8 did much to bolster the fortunes of the village.

In 1875 Philip Wootton of Boonton purchased the Old Boonton Tract from the Righter family for $10,000, and after taking in two partners, James Holmes and William G. Lathrop, sold the property to Messrs. Fitz Gibbon and Messer, of New York City, for $15,000 on April 5, 1880.[90]

The new owners erected a large paper mill on the site of the old forge, and carried on the manufacture of paper for something more than a decade.

Maurice Fitz Gibbon, a principal in the firm, moved his family first to nearby Ailanthus Hall (the former Polly Board House) in Parsippany, and later to the Ogden-Faesch mansion, where he resided at least during the summer seasons. He restored the mansion to a fine state of repair, with embellishments in the "Queen Ann Style" and with Victorian touches. His was the last family to occupy the historic mansion on its original site.[91]

In the late 1890's the Old Boonton Tract, along with other properties in that vicinity, including the Poor Farm, was acquired by the Jersey City Water Supply Company for purposes of a reservoir. Fitz Gibbon, who had obtained full title to the property, received $85,000 in compensation.[92] Part, if not all, of the old mansion was subsequently used in building the Glaab home on Malapardis Road in Whippany.

Preparations for the reservoir included the building of a great dam less than a mile downstream from Old Boonton, and the clearing of the reservoir basin of all buildings, structures, roads and trees. Only remnants of foundations and stone boundary walls were left in the basin, and a new bridge was built across the inlet to connect an extension of Washington Street of Boonton to the displaced road to Morristown. In the period 1902–3, after the dam was completed, the waters began to rise, and even the barren site of Old Boonton faded from view.

Birthplace of Boonton. Oil painting by Herbert T. Borgstrom from F. Wendt photo.

Chapter II

Boonton

1821–1861

Every community has a history which, if properly related, must be interesting and even important at least to those who belong to it. Here the fathers of such a community fought the battle of life, wrestled with the problems of moral responsibility, loved the living, pitied the sorrowful, helped the weak, wept over the dying; here they laid the foundation of a social fabric as best they could, often in a very blind but honest method, lived life as we now live it, and they died leaving their graves to us as silent monitors not to permit them to sink into forgetfulness. Although not as great as many who have lived, they are our forefathers, and the work they did for us merits a grateful record at our hands.*

In the late spring of 1860, John R. Chapin, artist and writer, visited Boonton for the purpose of writing a story on the ironworks at this place. The story, entitled "Among the Nail-Makers," was published in *Harper's New Monthly Magazine*, July 1860. Mr. Chapin's description of what he found here was written in excellent style, leaving the reader with a mental picture that helps to visualize the unusual location of the village and, using words with a deftness comparable to the brush strokes of a fine artist, he gives us the color and beauty of the scene. Herewith is a portion of Mr. Chapin's story:

> The village of Boonton is beautifully situated—so far as a charming prospect is concerned—upon the—almost precipitous—face of a bluff, which forms one of the sides of a deep ravine through which the Rockaway River empties its waters

*Rev. Joseph Farrand Tuttle, D.D., LL.D. Rockaway Presbyterian Church, 1847–1862; president, 1862-1892, Wabash College, Crawfordsville, Indiana.

into the plain below. It takes its name from a hamlet in the plain about a mile distant (now called "Old Boonton"), where was situated, at the period of the Revolution, a forge and furnace for the manufacture of the ore from Hibernia, Mount Hope, and Dickerson mines into "blooms" or square blocks of iron, which were afterward rolled into bars and sheets. The principal part of the town lies on the eastern face of the bluff, the houses rising one above another in successive terraces, thus affording to each a most delightful view over the valley and the distant hills for many miles. The opposite side of the ravine is bold and rocky, and at the upper end the river falls over the rocks a distance of about thirty feet in a beautiful cascade, which at some seasons assumes the appearance of a

Boonton Falls.

mountain torrent. After circling and eddying over its rocky bed, now stopping to disport in some quiet pool, now darting around some huge boulder which in vain strives to impede its progress, and anon rushing impetuously over a miniature cascade, ever hymning its song to the appreciative ear, it descends to the valley where it resumes its quiet flow until it joins the Passaic. The natural beauties of the spot must have been majestic, and still very attractive; but the hand of improvement has cramped and confined them, and will eventually obliterate them. The canal, the road, and the works are all built upon the side of the ravine, and occupy a portion of what was formerly the bed of the river. There are those still living and engaged in the works who well remember when the site of the furnace and mills was but a mass of boulders which had been brought down by the torrent, or from which the soil had been washed by the impetuous waters; when the howl of the wolf was heard on the neighboring hills; and when but one house occupied the site of the now flourishing town, with its large and commodious hotel, its handsome churches, stores, and private residences. Less than thirty years ago the first step was taken toward developing the resources of the place. Its immense water power and other advantages early attracted attention, and an association under the title of the "East Jersey Iron Manufacturing Company" [New Jersey Iron Company], was chartered by the Legislature in 1829. The Morris Canal was cut though about the same time. A dam, erected above the falls, furnishes water to the canal, which is drawn off at several points and, being conducted through the various buildings where power is required, finally finds its way back into the canal below the plane. The canal has a fall of two hundred feet, eighty of which are overcome by a single track plane of eight hundred feet in length, and the balance by means of locks. After repairing to the hotel, where they shook the dust off their feet, and washed their hands of life on the canal with its profanity, vulgarity and misery, Tint [Chapin] and his companion [his younger brother] started out to gather new experiences among the nail-makers.

Passing down the road, which leads to a collection of low, one-story shanties, built against the hill on one side, and a long brick building containing stores and the offices of the Company on the other, on, through, and around the various

* Indian Rock, also called Big Rock, was a huge sloping rock reaching from the river's edge to a point high in the bank near the Morris Canal. This description by Chapin was written before the Arch Bridge was erected in 1866 with stone from the Rock. The railroad spur was cut through the Rock in 1867. The stone taken from it was used in building the No. 2 blast furnace for the mill in 1868.

buildings composing the mills, they came at last, at the head of the ravine, to an irregular mass of rock, some fifteen or twenty feet in height, which seemed, like a screen, to shut out further progress. An irregular footpath led through a crevice, however, and up this they scrambled, to find themselves at length among a group of pines which grew upon the upper surface of the mass, their roots wringing a scanty subsistence from the soil which had accumulated there. A mossy carpet of the deepest emerald yielded to the pressure of their feet, and a rustic seat, erected by some considerate hand at the further perpendicular edge, afforded an excellent view of the fall, which was seen at the extreme upper edge of the ravine. A light cloud of spray rose in front of it, which as it was caught by a ray of the departing sunlight, assumed the prismatic colors, and added a ravishing charm to the otherwise wild and gloomy aspect of the spot. Elevated some twenty feet above the stream, our friends looked down upon a projecting spur of a rock that jutted out from the right, forcing the whole volume of water through a narrow gorge not more than three feet in width. Between this rock and the fall the stream pursued a languid course, forming several basins which, like polished mirrors, reflected the foaming cascade and the dark sides of the chasm, as well as the clear blue of the sky above, where the foliage allowed the light to struggle through. Here and there, on the surface of the rocks lying in the bed of the river, were several of those "pockets" or bowl-like formations noticed at the Clinton forge, one of which, on being measured, proved to be two feet six inches across and eighteen inches deep.

After sketching this delightful spot our friends, with lingering steps, turned away to the contemplation of the more utilitarian mills and the process of manufacturing iron so extensively carried on.

This scene, so aptly described by John Chapin, has been the stimulus of many moments of thought of a nostalgic nature. There remains, however, the consolation that time has been kind, and has not detracted from the natural beauty of the falls, the river, and the surrounding landscape.

A Town is Born

Although it is my intention to give a word picture of Boonton during the years of the Civil War, it will be helpful first to review the history of Boonton and how the Town came into being. This will allow us to approach the period of the war gradually, and review the events and problems which confronted our people.

For a point of beginning I have chosen the early 1820's. This period seems to be the transition point of Old Boonton, now covered by the Jersey City reservoir, and present Boonton as it is located today. There may be cause to wonder why the site was selected in the first place, on the side of a hill or mountain as some chose to call it, but we will learn that it was done of necessity rather than choice, for the idea of selecting an ideal spot for a community certainly never occurred to those responsible.

A major problem of that day was the shortage of fuel. A large number of forges and furnaces that dated back to the early colonial days were now idle and had fallen into a state of disuse, not because of the lack of demand for the product of these establishments, or the availability of the iron ore that abounded in the hills beyond Boonton, but because of the shortage of the fuel that was used in the processing of the iron in all its varied forms.

The fuel of this period was charcoal, and the charcoal was produced by felling trees and cutting them up into suitable lengths to be piled and covered with sod and earth, then to be fired up to burn very slowly in such a manner as to produce a fuel of high carbon content and the ability to produce sufficient heat to melt the iron from the stone. These charcoal pits can still be detected back in the hills as large depressions in the earth, the black soil evidencing the product manufactured there. The charcoal was then transported in large wagons made for the purpose to the manufactories and there consumed, hundreds of bushels used for each "heat" of the furnace.

The fuel situation was a serious problem. The wooded tracts nearby were fast reaching the point of depletion and it meant that fuel would have to come from sources much farther away. This brought about thoughts of a new means of transportation.

The Morris Canal

During the year of 1821, George P. McCulloch, a prominent citizen of Morristown, while sitting in a boat fishing on Lake Hopatcong, first conceived this revolutionary idea and foresaw the possibilities of a new mode of transportation for this area, the Morris Canal.[93] Here was an idea that when consummated would connect Easton on the Delaware with Jersey City on the eastern seaboard. It would mean the development of the iron and other interests in this State, and it would also be the means of bringing in a fuel to supplant the depleted charcoal supply. This fuel was anthracite coal.

A complete description of the Morris Canal would be lengthy and time consuming, and would very well distract from the principal concern, so our reference to it will be brief. The canal was constructed during the years 1825 to 1831

House of Tunis Peer. This house, more commonly known as the Cookerow house, was the starting point in the survey of William Scott's new road to Powerville, in 1822. The house was located on the easterly side of the Main Street bridge crossing Rte. 287.

from Phillipsburg to Newark, and then to Jersey City by 1836.[94] In planning the canal, some thought was given to a route that, on leaving Rockaway, would veer to the south to include Morristown in its course, and then on toward Newark. The lack of large feeder streams necessary for the operation of locks and planes and the difficulty of crossing or circumventing the mountains between Morristown and Newark must have been the deciding factor in the decision to choose the route through Boonton. The adequate supply of water from the Rockaway, Pompton and Passaic Rivers with their tributaries must have helped in this decision. Had this route not been taken, or if the canal had not been built at this

Boonton Plane and Lower Level

Canal Co. currency.

27

time, Boonton as it is located today may never have been developed, and would have remained a picturesque spot in the Jersey hills, with its falls and scenery undisturbed.

At this point in our story we meet William Scott, who just prior to 1822 purchased the Old Boonton Tract[95] and, at considerable expense, had a new road opened and graded leading through the tract on the east side of the river and near the falls, toward his gristmill and forge at Powerville.[96] This no doubt was prompted by a desire to bring notice to the fine water power available here. That road is our Main Street today, except for the portion that parallels Plane Street, Plane Street being included in William Scott's new road. It might be well to mention that William Scott's brother, Colonel John Scott, was taking an active interest in the canal project with George P. McCulloch.

Headed west toward Powerville

As it was necessary for the Canal Company to obtain a right of way through the numerous properties along its course, they obtained a deed from William Scott for such land required, and the privilege of damming the river above the falls, so that the

Gatehouse used to regulate flow of water from river into the canal. Also entrance to Lock No. 11 near Pond Bridge

canal might be fed at this place. In return the Canal Company granted him the privilege of using the canal as a raceway for conveying water to be converted into power in the event mills were built in the valley. The only stipulation was that the water be returned to the canal at the lower level, which was agreed. John L. Kanouse, who wrote of this in 1881 for Munsell's *History of Morris County*, stated that this was a master stroke of policy on the part of Scott; it no doubt aided him very much in disposing of this water power, and added largely to the value of the adjoining two hundred acres of land for which he received $5,000.[97] This two hundred acres consisted of all the land east of the canal, from about William Street to the vicinity of Highland Avenue, back over the hill as far as Wootton Street, and running to a sharp point near the top of Sheep Hill. It was purchased early in 1829, by David Wetmore and wife from William Scott,[98] and almost immediately was transferred to the New Jersey Iron Company,[99] a syndicate in New York that had plans for building an ironworks at this location. Also, they purchased a ten and one-half acre tract from Daniel T. Peer, which was the property on which the mills were erected in the valley.

Ironworks Constructed—English Pioneers

The erection of the ironworks was commenced in the fall of 1829 and it was completed to the extent that the first iron was rolled in May, 1831. The first machinery was imported from England and arrived June 10, 1830. The first workmen,

Philip Wootton

puddlers and rollers also came from England in June, 1830.[100] According to the account written by Miss Cora E. Hammond,* there were fifty-eight passengers in the first boat load. Among them were: Mr. and Mrs. Philip Wootton and daughter Ellen; Mr. and Mrs. Wilson and their children, Emma and Sarah; John Hodgkins and two of his children, Lavina and James; James Taylor and wife; and James and Ben Norton, brothers. Next year, 1831, these families came: Thomas Hammond and wife, with two sons, Enoch and Thomas; Mrs. John Hodgkins and four children, Thomas, Mary, Betsey and Sarah. On the first boat a cow was brought along to furnish milk for the babies, and sheep to supply fresh meat on the voyage.[101]

George Esten

Among the pioneers in the ironworks was George W. Esten. His coming here was in answer to an unusual request. The manager of the company, William Green, when in New York City, had asked for a man who could take entire charge of the pattern shop and carpenter work at the mills at Boonton, and to assist in establishing a church and Sunday School here. George W. Esten was suggested for the job, and in 1830, at the age of twenty-three years, he began his long service in our community.[102] Mr. Esten started Sunday Schools in Boonton, Powerville and Rockaway Valley, superintending each one. He identified himself with the Presbyterian Church, and afterward became associated with the First Congregational Society,[103] holding its meetings in a little building located on Main Street, a short distance down the hill from William Street. This was known as the "Free Church," due to its activities with the abolitionist movement. Mr. Esten was eighty-one years old when he died, July 26, 1889.

A number of homes were built for the employees; these were erected under the hill on lower Plane Street. One of the original

* A teacher at School St. School in the early 1900's

31

buildings was torn down during the 1960's. It was located at 127 Plane Street. A larger building was erected on the east side of Main Street, opposite the falls. This building was used as a boarding house.[104] In somewhat later years it was renovated and owned by Theodore Ringlieb. The pond nearby, that was formed by the damming of the river, was called "Boardinghouse Pond" by the early inhabitants of this place.

Religious Interests

The first settlers of Boonton were not negligent in providing means for religious instruction. Meetings were held under the large oaks that formed a grove where the Presbyterian Church now stands, and in private dwellings. Later, in 1832, they were held in the newly erected schoolhouse. The first church

First Presbyterian Church at Boonton. This building was erected on the east side of Church Street in 1832. When the present church was erected in 1860 the little church was sold and moved across the street. it was called Washington Hall and was used for public meetings, etc.

First Presbyterian Church (1860).

organization was formed July 1, 1832, with the title "Church at Boonton," and later that year they passed a resolution to erect a house of worship. The following minute was copied from the record and inserted in a Manual for the members of the First

Presbyterian Church, Boonton Falls, New Jersey: "In order to proceed lawfully and obtain a charter they found it necessary to assume some specific name. Accordingly, on the tenth of Dec., A.D., 1832, at a public meeting of the church, duly called for the purpose, the question was proposed: 'By what name shall this Church be hereafter called?' After mature deliberation, the Confession of Faith of the Presbyterian Church being read, and its doctrines being assented to by all the members, it was unanimously resolved "That this Church shall be known as the 'First Presbyterian Church of Boonton.'" [105] The cornerstone of the present church was laid in June, 1859, and the dedication took place May 12, 1860. Rev. Daniel E. Megie was the Pastor during the Civil War years.

The history of the Roman Catholic faith in Boonton goes back beyond the founding of a parish here. In the absence of a formal church organization, the Catholics in Boonton made pilgrimages to the church at "Bottle Hill," now called Madison. The leader of Catholicism in Boonton was John Hyland, who came from Ireland in 1829, and soon afterward made the acquaintance of John McCarthy, who was a superintendent in the ironworks. Services were held in the McCarthy home until 1842 and later they were held in the home of John Hyland, who lived in 124 Liberty Street. In 1846 a plot of ground was given by the Company and in 1847 a small wooden church was erected on the knoll opposite the present church. As the mills and village grew, the parish outgrew the little church, and when the Rev. Dominic Castet was appointed rector on January 16, 1860, he soon after urged the building of the present church. Bishop James Roosevelt Bayley, who was the first Bishop of New Jersey, having been appointed in 1853, with the entire state as his diocese, officiated at the laying of the cornerstone of this new church, September 16, 1860. The church was called "Our Lady of Mt. Carmel," as is noted in the "Metropolitan Catholic Almanac of 1861" where the following appears: "Boonton, Morris County, New Jersey, Our Lady of Mt. Cannel, Rev. D. Castet."[106] The little wooden church was moved intact to Upper Hibernia; it was called "St. Patrick's" and served that parish

34

Our Lady of Mt. Cannel Church (1860).

until its destruction by fire in 1910. It may be well to include an interesting note connected with the present church. This occurred in 1862, and probably refers to the scaffolding used in decorating the interior of the church. The following is to Andrew Bell Cobb, of Parsippany:

Boonton, April 14th, 1862.

Sir,

I do not know whether the scaffolding poles used in my new church belong to you or to Mr. Martin Walsh. Supposing they are yours, I would buy them from you. Would you be so kind as to send me word by the return of the Boonton stage this evening, and tell me how much you want for them.

Yours respectfully,
Rev. D. C. Castet[107]

A. B. Cobb, Esq.

School Street School (1852). Right Wing 1864–66. Left Wing 1869–70

The Early Schools

The first school in Boonton was held in part of a dwelling house which stood on Plane Street, at the foot of the hill, about opposite where the Bethel A.M.E. Church now stands. The New Jersey Iron Company furnished the building and paid the salary of the teacher, who was a Miss Dean. The following year, 1832, a new school was erected at Cedar and Liberty Streets, and the school moved to that location. If you look at the gables of the building, now used as a residence, you will see the trim of the gable with its scrolled edge. This detail was frequently used on schools of that period.

In the year 1850, under an act of Legislature to establish free schools, the people of Boonton, following the recommendations of the township superintendent of public schools, John L. Kanouse, presented the proposition of free schools at a public meeting for that purpose. The proposition being favorably received, a petition was drafted and presented to the next Legislature. It was passed and went into effect immediately. Under this act, in April, 1851, William

St. Mary's School (1910).

Lathrop, James Holmes and George W. Esten were elected the first Board of Trustees. During that year the New Jersey Iron Company donated a plot of ground at the present School Street School site; there a brick building of suitable size, two stories in height, was erected and completed the early part of the following year. School was opened in it on July 19, 1852. This was the first, and for many years the only free school in Morris County. An addition, toward Main Street, was added to the school in 1864–66; and a second addition, toward Birch Street, was built in 1869–70.[108] The addition toward Main Street was removed to make space for the school building that was erected in 1897 (and demolished in 1967).*

The first school of the parish for Our Lady of Mount Carmel was established in 1860 by the Rev. Dominic Castet in the church basement. Father Castet and his successor, the Rev. Louis Gambosville, taught with the aid of a lay faculty which included John Holland, the inventor of the modern submarine. In 1876, when the local economy collapsed, the

---

* The section on John L. Kanouse contains further information on public schools.

parochial school was reluctantly closed. The public school could accommodate pupils from the first three grades only, so that for many children formal education was ended. The boys and young men who were eager to continue their studies gathered in the rectory evenings for personal instruction by Father Gambosville.

When conditions improved in the 1880's, the pastor, the Rev. J. P. Poels, invited the Sisters of Saint Dominic of Caldwell, New Jersey, to assume charge of the religious and secular education in the parish. A convent was built on the east corner of Birch and Oak Streets and the Sisters arrived on September 1, 1887. For four years they taught long hours in the basement of the church, instructing the children by day and holding adult education classes at night. In 1891 a parochial building was erected on the west corner of Birch and Oak Streets, housing four-room St. Mary's School; on the second floor was St. Joseph's Hall, which was used as a school auditorium and a parish social center.[109] This building was torn down in 1961.

Furnaces and Nail Factory

With the increasing of the facilities at the ironworks, the first blast furnace was built in 1833, and charcoal was used for fuel. The canal, now in use, brought in the charcoal from sources miles away. This furnace consumed one thousand bushels of charcoal per day and produced thirty-five tons of pig iron per week. It was not until 1848 that the first anthracite furnace was built, and in 1868 the second furnace was erected. The first anthracite furnace was erected under the supervision of a Samuel Thomas, of Catasauqua, Pa.

Though only twenty-seven years old at the time, he constructed and successfully put into blast Boonton's first anthracite furnace. This furnace had a capacity to produce five thousand tons of pig iron per year. About six months later in the fall of 1848, Mr. Thomas returned to Pennsylvania and the

Boonton Ironworks.

supervision of the furnace was given to George Jenkins until his death in 1864, when his son, Henry C. Jenkins, succeeded him. These were prosperous days, for during the war years there were more than five hundred men employed. The amount paid monthly in wages was about $30,000.

The New Jersey Iron Company decided to add the manufacture of cut nails to its business in 1848, and the following year erected a building 50 feet by 150 feet near the head of the inclined plane. This was called the upper nail factory and it was in full operation by the fall of 1851.

Although the expansion of the ironworks was generally considered continuous, it did experience some difficulties during the years of 1845 to 1852. This was due primarily to the dropping of the market, and also to careless management of the affairs of the Company. In 1845, William Green, Jr., succeeded Henry Brevoort in the superintendency of the Boonton Works, and it was about this time that Mr. Green sent for his nephew, William G. Lathrop, to come to Boonton to assist in straightening out the books of the Company.[110]

Blast Furnace at Boonton. This furnace erected by Samuel Thomas, 1848. Photo by Victor Prevost. Circa 1854. George Eastman House Collection.

Upper Nail Factory, circa 1854. Photo by Victor Prevost. George Eastman House Collection.

William Gerard Lathrop.

William G. Lathrop

William G. Lathrop was born October 29, 1812, at Norwich, Connecticut. As a young man of about thirty-three years, he was living in retirement on a farm outside of Rahway, N.J., having been quite successful as the junior partner of

Talbot & Lathrop, New York, importers of Chinese and foreign products. Lathrop had arrived in Boonton in 1845 at the request of his uncle, William Green, superintendent of the New Jersey Iron Company. Also, at this time in 1845, John Hill came to Boonton from Catskill, New York, and accepted the position of paymaster at the Ironworks. We will learn more about John Hill as our story continues.

To aid Mr. Lathrop in determining the ownership of the various properties sold by the Company, the Company commissioned Burnett, Serrell & Co., Civil Engineers in New York City, to survey all the land originally owned by the Company, and draft a map that would show the properties held, transferred, etc. This map of Boonton, always referred to as the Serrell Map of 1848, was the first map to show the streets of Boonton, and on each lot the name of the owner was entered as ownership was established. Unfortunately, there is nothing to show the date of title. Mr. Green made sure his family names were remembered, for we have a Green Street, a Cornelia Street, and a William Street, the last two bearing the given names of his wife and himself.

When William Green retired in 1850, William Lathrop succeeded his uncle in the position of superintendent, continuing to serve in that capacity a total of 26 years until the works closed down in 1876. After the closing he was placed in charge by the Executors of the estate of J. Couper Lord to look after matters and keep the works in repair, which he continued to do until his retirement in 1880.

In 1869, William Lathrop became the chairman of the Board of Trustees, as the governing body of the Town of Boonton was then called, and the Serrell Map was adopted as the official map of the Town of Boonton. A copy of this map is on file in the Morris County Records Office. The original Serrell Map of 1848 is now in the hands of the writer, waiting for our Town to have a suitable repository for historical items of this nature. At that time this map will be presented to the Town in the name of Harry Gordon, uncle of Homer Dixon.

It was their forethought to preserve this map for future generations.[111]

In 1872, Mr. Lathrop built a massive masonry residence on the street that bears his name. He insisted that all who worked on it be residents of Boonton, thereby helping the unemployed of the Town. He lived there until his death in 1882 at the age of 70. His residence, with its extensive grounds, became the New Jersey State Firemen's Home in 1900.[112]

Fuller and Lord

The year 1852 saw a change in the ownership of the mills. The new owner was Dudley B. Fuller, and shortly after he was joined by James Couper Lord as a partner, under the firm name of Fuller & Lord.[113] The market had become more favorable and prices for their products increased. As a result the mill thrived. A new nail factory was built below in the area where the Town garage is now located. Facilities were increased, additional buildings were erected and important repairs and alterations made, all tending to increase the efficiency and production of the Works.

Description of the Works

John L. Kanouse in writing his contribution to Munsell's History of Morris County inventories the Works as follows:

> There are in the large mill twelve double puddling furnaces, seven large heating furnaces, and two rotary and crocodile squeezers. The average production of puddle bars was three hundred and twenty tons per week. The nut mill contained four furnaces and four nut machines. In the two nail factories there were one hundred and fifty nail machines with a capacity of producing, when run to the full extent, 200,000 kegs of nails per year. There were in the saw mill three sets of stave machines with the capacity of 20,000

Boonton Ironworks (1864). Photo gift of Marion Prall

staves per day. For this, 1,000 cords of chestnut logs were required each year, and for making headings about 400,000 feet of whitewood and pine boards. The staves were piled in sheds to season thoroughly before they were used in the cooper shop. Over 2,000,000 staves and over 900,000 hoops were used in turning out annually an average of 150,000 kegs. From seventy to eighty kegs were considered a fair product for ten hours work, although some young experts have been known to turn out one hundred to one hundred twenty in ten hours. The mills, furnaces, foundry and various shops and storehouses cover fully six acres of grounds.

As a motive power for this vast concern, 1500 horsepower was required, and was derived from four large overshot wheels, six turbines and three steam engines. Besides these mills the company operated several valuable iron mines and altogether gave employment to over five hundred hands.[114]

Growth of Boonton

Along with the growth of the Ironworks, the population of the village increased and houses were built over the hillside for the workers and their families. Many of them owned their homes, buying lots from the Iron Company for $10 to $25 and, if they needed, they could borrow money against their wages to erect the houses thereon.[115] Thus the village had grown, and as shown by the census of 1860, the village of Boonton had 419 families, living in 326 dwellings, with a population of 2,230. The value of real estate was $790,725; the value of personal property was $175,700, or a total of $966,425. Boonton's population had increased by 800 in those last five years.[116]

Bridges

Although Boonton had advanced considerably in 1860, it was still necessary to go to Powerville or Old Boonton to cross the river. In November 1861 the first bridge was built across the Pond in West Boonton. This body of water covered a larger area prior to the building of the bridge. The level of the water was the same as it is now, and it extended almost to the point where Essex Avenue and West Main Street meet. As one studies the contour of the green at the Grace Lord Monument, and imagines the amount of fill that was used to bring Main Street to its present level, it becomes evident that the Pond was reduced considerably in area by the approaches to the bridge. The first Pond Bridge, or "New Bridge" as it was then called, was of wooden construction, and narrower in width; it was about five feet lower than the present bridge and the approach to it, on the West Boonton end, was quite steep. The cost of this bridge was about $1,600.[117]

In 1867–8, the first Morris Avenue Bridge, or Silk Mill Bridge, as it was later called, was built. It was of wood and stone construction and cost about $1,000. The last bridge to span the river at this point was removed with the building of Route 287 in 1962.[118]

The description of our bridges would not be complete without including the Arch Bridge and the "Lover's Lane" leading to it. Through the years this beautiful landmark, in its

Arch Bridge.

sylvan setting, has been the subject for many artists and photographers. Although it is more often remembered because of its romantic aspect, its purpose was for reasons material and essential. The Ironworks had laid water mains throughout the mill property for fire protection. This system was supplied by a pipe from the Morris Canal at the rear of the blast furnaces. But there were times when the canal was drained of its water for repairs, etc., and this would place the mills in a vulnerable position to fire. In 1866 the Arch Bridge was constructed as a viaduct to carry a large iron pipe that was laid from the Pond, down Lover's Lane, and across the Arch

Bridge, to furnish a constant water supply for fire protection and other purposes. This rugged but picturesque structure of cut stone was the work of John Carson, Sr., and remains a monument to a master craftsman. When the bridge was nearing completion and large stones were being placed at the approach near Indian Rock, Mr. Carson was injured by a premature blast that had been set to break the stone. Several months later he died, his injuries contributing to his death.[119]

Indian Rock. This rock mass originally reached down to the river edge and was cut away for the bridge approach. Also, it reached high to the right into the canal bank. The rock was cut away to permit the railroad spur to go near to the falls and return over a trestle to bring the ore, coal, etc., to the rear of the blast furnaces. The stone removed was shaped for use in building the Arch Bridge and the No. 2 Blast Furnace.

Dr. John Grimes—Anti-Slavery Activities

In thinking of Boonton and its problems during the days from its inception and through the years that included the Civil War we realize our town was not unlike other communities throughout the North. The people gave thought to the

Dr. John Grimes.

problems of the day and expressed themselves in varied ways
and degree. The question of slavery and its abolition was a topic
that caused some friends to become enemies, and those who
were recognized as leaders in such activities were either supported or ostracized depending on the feelings of the people. Dr.
John Grimes was an outstanding example of this leadership.

His participation in and his dedication to the cause of abolition were the basis of numerous tales and stories told about
him by his contemporaries, some of them singing his praises

and others condemning him for his convictions. The nature of the remarks was influenced and colored by associations and opinions, political, religious and otherwise, of the individuals relating the stories. These stories have survived through the years, and to this day there are those who refer to Dr. Grimes as being a very "queer" person probably because, among other reasons, he was a vegetarian who attempted to encourage others by sponsoring vegetarian dinners and meetings in Liberty Hall which he had erected on Main Street, near the corner of Liberty Street. Among his critics were those who had selfishly thought only of themselves and could not comprehend a man who would suffer pecuniary loss and abuse because of ideals and principles he thought to be right. It was primarily his efforts and associations with the Abolitionist movement that attracted notice to Dr. Grimes and caused him to become such a controversial figure.

Dr. Grimes built Liberty Hall about 1844, or just prior thereto. He must have deemed the building of this hall a necessity, considering the difficulties he encountered in trying to obtain facilities for large gatherings. When this meeting place was completed, Dr. Grimes refused no one the use of its conveniences. Read what Isaac Lyon, a writer of that day, had to say about Liberty Hall:

> Our so-called "Old Liberty Hall," built and owned by Dr. John Grimes, is the oldest public hall in the village, and for many years was the only one. This renowned old hall stands on Main, near Liberty Street, and when filled to its utmost capacity will hold about 400 persons. The fame of this grand old hall is widespread—yea, almost world-wide—and its doors have been entered by most of the people of Boonton and the surrounding country. It has been used at one time and another for almost every conceivable purpose, both of a public and private character. It well deserves to be called Liberty Hall, for within its walls almost every description of performances have been enacted. Song and dance, feast and frolic—wedding and funeral—show and concert—music and

rejoicing—history and drama—farce and tragedy—debate and disputation upon things seen and unseen—literature and science—slavery and anti-slavery—republicanism and democracy—whigism, know-nothingism, and all the other "isms" ever heard or dreamed of—politics and religion—patriotism and free-soilism—spirit rappings and vegetarianism—woman's rights and woman's wrongs, in all their various phases and ramifications,—free suppers, free speech and free everything—all have been enacted, seen, heard and listened to, time and again within its venerable and time hallowed walls. Long may the flag of the free and brave float in triumph from the battlements of our famous old Liberty Hall! May its foundations endure for a thousand years yet to come, and may its shadows never be less than they are at the present moment![120]

Do we detect an attempt at humor, or does it have a tinge of the ridicule to which Dr. Grimes had grown so accustomed? Probably it was just Isaac Lyon's inimitable style. However, let us start from the beginning.

Dr. Grimes was born in Parsippany in the year 1802. He was the son of Jonathan Casper Grimes, a farmer and blacksmith in the Halseytown area of Parsippany, and Hulda Leonard of Pine Brook.[121] It was not by mere coincidence that Dr. Grimes was to become involved in the Abolitionist movement, for his father, Jonathan Casper Grimes, was a fearless, outspoken advocate of the anti-slavery movement before him.

Dr. Grimes as a boy was educated in the rural schools of the area, and any reference to a formal education has not been found; however, in 1824 he decided to embrace the medical profession as his life's work. He studied medicine under the tutelage of Dr. Stephen Fairchild,[122] of Parsippany, and at the age of twenty-six he received his certificate, being found a competent person to practice medicine.

The *History of Morris County* (Lewis—1914) describes the procedure for becoming a doctor. It was the custom of that period that a student aspiring to become a doctor would first make application to some practicing physician with whom be desired to study. The preceptor would then deposit the application with the Morris District Medical Society, as the local medical society was called at that time. After four years of study, the student would be examined by the Censors of the Society and, if found satisfactory to them, a license to practice medicine would be granted.[123]

Dr. Grimes began to practice medicine in the village of Newfoundland, New Jersey, in 1828. He served that community for nearly five years before establishing himself in Boonton.[124]

With his coming to Boonton in 1833, he could be considered one of the pioneers of this place, but his acceptance by the community was not exactly a warm one. It seemed that he was on the unpopular side of nearly every public question, of politics, religion, temperance and diet, as we will learn later.

It was said he became the first president of the Anti-Slavery Society in the State of New Jersey, but the office of secretary seems to be more correct. The headquarters for a time were situated in Boonton. He published and edited Boonton's first newspaper, *The Monthly Advertiser*, in 1843. This paper lasted but a few editions. He then published the *New Jersey Freeman*, during the years 1844 to 1850. Both newspapers served as the organ of the Anti-Slavery Society and contained very little local news. They were used to propagate the Abolitionist movement, to tell of the hardships of the Negro slaves, and also to extol the virtues of temperance.

The bold, outspoken stand taken by Dr. Grimes subjected him to the severest persecution. He was maligned and ill-treated by almost everyone, but actuated by what he considered a principle, the advice of friend or the threat of enemy could not deter him in the least.[125]

Among the references pertaining to Dr. Grimes found in local histories, one in particular commands further attention. In the appendix of Isaac S. Lyon's *Historical Discourse on Boonton*, 1873, Mr. Lyon tells of Dr. Grimes and the first book printed in Boonton. Dr. Grimes had a small, crude printing press, used mostly for turning out billheads, labels, etc. It was on this press that Dr. Grimes set up and printed a book of forty-eight pages, entitled *Right and Wrong in Boonton, No. 1*. This book or booklet contained the report of a committee of the Anti-Slavery group in Boonton, summarizing their meetings, the obstacles and problems the Abolitionists were confronted with, and covered a period from 1834 to the date of the report, May 24, 1840. The report was printed by Dr. Grimes shortly thereafter.

An original copy of the book was found in the Special Collections at Rutgers University Library, and a duplicate was made for the writer's convenience. To fully describe the nature of *Right and Wrong in Boonton, No. 1*, and convey to the reader a comprehensible explanation for its being written, presents a problem due to the principals involved, namely the Anti-Slavery Society and the Presbyterian Church of Boonton. The approach to this problem demanded considerable thought and deliberation, for on the one hand we have a printed document in which we find a complete report of the proceedings of the Anti-Slavery Society and their grievances against the First Presbyterian Church at Boonton; while on the other hand we find no printed word or reference offering a refutation or defense against the charges made, placing the church at a complete disadvantage to start with.

It should be pointed out, however, that there was one exception to be taken to the statements made by the Anti-Slavery Society in their booklet. It states on page twenty-eight of the booklet that the Session Book, the record of the actions of the Session of the Church, was mutilated by tearing from it all record of a certain case in question. This was not the truth, for I, having the opportunity to read and inspect this old Session Book on September 16, 1962, found it to be intact with no signs whatever of pages having been torn from it. This was a lesson in itself, for it is a common thing to accept old books, diaries, etc., as bonafide references just because they happened to be written by someone of that day.

The general structure of the Abolitionist movement wasn't new or something that was conceived in Dr. Grimes' day. The noted John Woolman, born of Quaker parents in Mt. Holly, New Jersey, over one hundred years before Dr. Grimes, is considered by many as the founder of the movement. He became a Quaker preacher at the age of twenty-three, and he also advocated vegetarianism and temperance. As early as 1753 he published in Philadelphia a paper entitled "Some Considerations on the Keeping of Negroes." So we find a distinct parallel in the lives of the two men. Surely Dr. Grimes must have admired the efforts of John Woolman, and he could very easily be considered a disciple of the Quaker preacher, striving for the betterment of his fellow-man.[126]

As to the attitude of the Church and its followers, in reference to slavery, this was also influenced by thoughts and decisions pronounced many years before by the tribunals of the Church, and had much to do with the actions that were taken. The Presbyterian General Assembly, in session in 1794, adopted a note to one of the questions in its Longer Catechism, affirming the biblical condemnation of "man-stealers," as all who are concerned in bringing any of the human race into slavery or retaining them therein. Stealers of men are those who bring off slaves or freemen, and keep, sell, or buy them, etc." But this note was erased by the General Assembly in 1816, in a resolve that characterized slavery as a mournful evil, but does not direct that the churches be purged of it. And, though the Synod of Kentucky in 1835 adopted a report which condemned slave-holding broadly and thoroughly, the same report admitted that "those who hold to our Communion are involved in it," and no action was taken requiring a choice between their connection with the church and their activity in buying, holding and selling slaves.[127]

In attempting to understand fully the position of the local Church in this controversy, we must delve into the problems and situations that were a definite influence on the thinking of the people.

There were those who held positions in a supervisory capacity at the mills who were unyielding in their vehement denunciation of the Abolitionists and their principles. The mills, along with many northern manufacturers, had been shipping their wares to the southern market which no doubt was a source of great income. They felt that if the Abolitionists continued with their agitation to abolish slave labor, and were successful in their endeavors, it could only lead to the loss of that market by the northern capitalists and the possibility of the South entering into a free-trade pact with England and other sources of supply, thereby putting an end to the steady stream of wealth that had been pouring in during the years prior to the war.

One might ask, "What possible connection could all this have with the Church?" It must be agreed that the churches were the largest organizations in the village and certainly were a great influence on the people.

Munsell's *History of Morris County*, in describing the activities of John Jacob Faesch, had this to say regarding his connection with the Rockaway Presbyterian Church: "Faesch is described as a very generous and large hearted man, but very aristocratic in his ideas. He gave liberally to the Church, so much that in a subscription made in 1781, a prominent man in the Rockaway congregation subscribed, 'as much as any in the parish except Esq. Faesch.' It is said, however, that he supported religion only as a means of keeping the lower classes in subjection." [128]

In 1889, Mary Harriott Norris, author of a book entitled *Dorothy Delafield*, brought to light in a disguised manner quite a bit of Boonton's history of the period in question. It is generally agreed that Miss Norris' book was not accepted as a literary gem, but it served its purpose. Although the names of persons and places were fictitious, the situations and parallels set forth by Miss Norris are accepted by the informed as being a fair description of life and activity in our town. Certainly she had a story to tell, and to protect herself,

Miss Norris used this novel form to do it.

To quote Miss Norris:

> The mills were managed by a corporation of "bosses-limited." These bosses were social leaders. There were boss-puddlers, boss-nailers, boss-plumbers, boss-coopers, even boss-laborers, and other bosses innumerable . . . A Quincyite sometimes said, with quiet humor, "About every third man in Quincy [Boonton] is a boss."

·   ·   ·

> The Presbyterian Church was a small pea-green structure, with a central tower containing a mellow, friendly bell. It had a great many brackets stuck under the eaves and about the porches, a town clock that rarely went, and a membership impregnable in the estimation of the Quincyites, since it gathered into its fold not only the bosses of the mills, but also, in an ex-officio way, the owners themselves, who were among the elect in a neighboring city.[129]

The foregoing quotes used from Miss Norris' book are not intended in a derogatory sense, but rather to help us better understand and justify the differences of opinion held by our citizens of that day. A social problem did exist, and its existence contributed greatly to the decisions the people had to make. Boonton was a one-industry town, and the livelihood of a large number of persons was dependent on the attitudes held by those in control of the mills.

The Anti-Slavery element met opposition from another source when they attempted to institute a "campaign of education." The federal administration tried to suppress it by permitting postmasters to remove newspapers, printed documents and like material from the mails. Mobs attacked abolition meetings and committed other acts of violence, while Congress from 1836 to 1844 enforced a "gag" rule forbidding any paper relating to slavery or its abolition to be received.[130]

An anticlimax was reached in the Boonton affair when in 1841, a number of men broke with the Presbyterian Church and, on April 19, 1841, the First Congregational Society of Boonton, New Jersey, was incorporated. Dr. John Grimes, George W. Esten, John Maxfield, James S. Norris and Daniel C. Norris were among those named in the Society. They met in a building located near the corner of William and Main Streets. It is shown on the Serrell map of 1848, near the curve in Main Street, and it was called the "Free Church." In Dr. Grimes' paper, *The New Jersey Freeman*, reference was always made to the "Free Church" and not to the "Congregational Society of Boonton." Just how long this Church existed is not known, and it is not at all improbable that the organization just appeared to dissolve.

This apparent dissolution was necessary, for if the Anti-Slavery movement was to be carried on successfully it would have to be done in extreme secrecy. The leaders in the movement had been harried by riot and violence; they were resisted by the clergy and the Church; they were repulsed by Congress and its gag rule; and now if they were to continue their activities they were liable to arrest and punishment. Therefore the need for extreme secrecy was imperative and with that secrecy came the "Underground Railroad."

The passage of the Fugitive Slave Law in September 1850 was received by the people of the State of New Jersey with more than passing interest. The feeling of resentment ran high, and the law was met with open defiance. In the Trenton-Philadelphia area the Society of Friends was assisting the runaway slaves to continue their journey north into New England and Canada, with hopes of consequent freedom. There were various routes by which these "fugitives" were spirited through the State, and three of them were principal routes over which at least 40,000 slaves were secretly conducted.

The success of the movement depended on the secrecy by which it operated. No one seemed to know who the leaders of this organization were; and no one knew how it procured its funds. One writer of that day described it as an enterprise where statistics were heretical and where know-nothingism was a religion.

The sympathizers who were active in its functions were harassed by persons who, although they were upholding the law as it was written, were classed as bounty hunters, and were despised by the groups of citizens who assisted the slaves in their bid for freedom. The attraction to the bounty hunter was the price on the head of the runaway slave. They received from $50 to $800 depending on the physical condition of the fugitive apprehended.

In its operation, however, the "Underground Railroad" presented no difficult problems for the slave except fear of detection. For this reason the "trains" of slaves were generally sent through New Jersey at night, resting by day in barns, in the recesses of the woods, in cellars, or even in the kitchens of the more enthusiastic members of the cause.[131]

The resistance movement against the law was very pronounced in the Boonton area and there must have been a change of opinions of some of our citizens, for we find Dr. Grimes and his fellow workers receiving greater recognition and cooperation in their struggle to help the oppressed. Among those connected with the Doctor in the underground movement were William C. Lathrop, John Hill, Thomas Willis, Philip Wootton, George Ely, Charles B. Norris, Frederick Stone, James Grimes, George Coates, Nathan Hopkins, and as a boy of fourteen years, Charles F. Hopkins, who later distinguished himself in the war to come.

Dr. Grimes' home was a "station" in the chain of stop-overs across our State. His father's home in Parsippany and the Powerville Hotel were also used at times. Charles Hopkins in writing of this described how he drove over the road through Rockaway Valley, Split Rock, Charlottesburg and Newfoundland during the night to deliver the load entrusted to him.[132] Such was the contribution of our supposedly "lawabiding" citizens in a controversy that eventually took a war to decide.

How rewarding and gratifying it must have been to Dr. Grimes when on January 1, 1863, President Abraham Lincoln issued that memorable document, "The Emancipation Proclamation." Dr. Grimes had given over thirty years to a cause in which he had explicit belief. The rigors of ceaseless hours spent in this crusade were not without their effect on his personal well-being. As a result of a long and serious illness he lost a leg in 1865 and shortly thereafter an arm. Notwithstanding these serious and trying drawbacks, he continued to act as a consulting physician and also managed his drug store located next to his home on the corner of Main and Liberty Streets.

Dr. John Grimes died September 12, 1875. His funeral was attended by many of his fellow townsmen; the service was conducted by the Rev. Henry A. Van Houten who, in 1838, bad succeeded Rev. Vance in the Presbyterian Church, and was not unknown by Dr. Grimes and his friends.[133]

Pre-War Politics

In attempting to complete the picture of Boonton just prior to the Civil War, perhaps we should review briefly the political situation of that period. The several factions within the Democratic Party, each insisting that their suggestions and contributions make up the framework of the platform they were to endorse, could not agree, with the result that the regular Democratic Party was split into three separate parties, each one nominating its own choice for presidential and vice-presidential candidates. On the other hand, the Republican Party, meeting in Chicago, enjoyed the solidarity that was to spell success and, on May 18, 1860, Abraham Lincoln of Illinois and Hannibal Hamlin of Maine were named the choice of the Republican Party.

With four presidential candidates in the field the results were inevitable. The Republicans carried their national ticket and even New Jersey, for the first time in twelve years, wavered in her allegiance to the Democratic Party, giving four electoral votes for Lincoln and Hamlin, and three for Douglas and Johnson. It was the only instance where the State had ever divided electoral votes.[134]

Morris County, although not as strongly Democratic as the majority of the counties in the State, was the scene of intense campaigning on both sides. Political clubs were organized which functioned with great energy to support their candidates.

"Old Pequannoc" was always in the political limelight because of the many close contests that took place when choosing leaders. In fact, one could say that it was a divided township, the eastern being predominantly Democratic and the western, or Boonton section, being strongly Republican. Although this intense rivalry existed, we will later find that the majority of our citizens forgot their differences and united to support the common cause.

The Republicans and others friendly to the Republican program met on August 18, 1860, at Liberty Hall, in Boonton, for the purpose of ratifying the nomination of Lincoln and Hamlin; the usual speeches and music were heard, and a Lincoln and Hamlin Club of over 100 members was organized. The following were named as officers: President, George Jenkins; Vice President, O. F. Gaines; Secretary, Edwin E. Willis; and Treasurer, John Hill.[135]

The Democrats of Pequannock Township were not at all satisfied with the course their party had taken, and when a fusion ticket was presented, they demurred and placed in the papers this notice, stating their intention and reasons for taking such action:

TO THE PUBLIC

We, the undersigned, voters of Pequannoc, who were sup-
porters of Fillmore and Donelson in 1856, and advocates of
Bell and Everett until a fusion was made with the
Breckenbridge and Douglas electoral tickets, for the purpose
of success, having been placed in a false position by such
fusion, desire to say to the public that we cannot support an
electoral ticket whose vote is to be determined by chance, nor
cooperate with men whose political principles we have
always opposed. How can we, as consistent men, go up to the
polls on the coming presidential election in November next,
and vote for this fusion ticket? Who would we help to elect
—our nominees, or the nominees of a party who are opposed
to us upon all the great national measures of the day? Would
it not be sacrificing all our former principles, and lending our
aid virtually to help restore peace and harmony and to
reunite, if possible, and bring together, the discordant elements
of a divided and corrupt party—a party that has already
existed too long by the pickings from the public crib? We
cannot fuse with such corrupt politicians as these, without
becoming infected with the same malady.

Were we to pursue such a course, how would we be the
advocates of Protection to American Labor, purity of the ballot
box, and safety of our American Institutions and
Government, by locking arms with a party who have always
been opposed to us, and strong advocates of free trade to the
injury of American labor? How would such a course tend to
displace from power, in our State, a party that has abused the
power it held so long, and by its reckless course of legislation
brought it to a state of bankruptcy? Only a few years ago the
financial condition of our State was sound and prosperous—
now it is bankrupt. And it had grown so with a current revenue
sufficient, if judiciously managed, to meet all the necessary
expenses. Under existing circumstances we feel compelled, as
a second choice, to give our votes to Lincoln, believing his
sterling honesty to be such that the Constitution will be the
basis of all his actions, more than the principles of the
Republican party.[136]

Richard Speer	Abraham Brown
Martin VanNess	Jacob Berry
Stephen Post	Paul DeBow
Peter J. C. Mead	John P. DeBow
Robert H. Mead	James J. Mandeville
Peter Berry	Henry H. Berry
Henry C. DeBow	Hugh Heath
Adrian Mandeville	Peter J. Roome
Garret C. DeMott	Ralph Cooper
John DeMott	Abraham Cooper
Nathan DeMott	G. J. Jacobus
Samuel DeMott	James D. Jacobus
Halmagh Mandeville	Abraham C. Miller
Abraham J. Mandeville	Jesse Gaines
Thomas A. Mandeville	Wm. L. Gladson
Henry DeMott	Daniel Peer

"Wide-Awakes"

With all this political activity occurring, the citizens of Boonton were not forgetting the main issues that were threatening the Country, and on September 9, 1860, the organization of a "Wide-Awake" unit was announced. These "Wide-Awake" units were organized in most of the larger communities and were a sort of Home Guard or Minute Man Company organized for the purpose of local protection.

Boonton's was headed by Capt. Edwin Bishop, who had charge of the machine shop at the Ironworks. A full complement of officers was appointed and it had a membership of about eighty men, all uniformed and equipped at their own expense. A proud group of men they were, with their plain but neat uniforms, consisting of the New York Seventh grey suit, black sleeve cuffs, collar and pantaloon stripes, white body and cross belts and high regulation hat with pompom. Capt. Bishop had served in the New York Seventh, so the choice of uniform is quite obvious.

This Company was later known as the "Boonton National Guard," and the men drilled several evenings a week at the mill and in Independence Hall, to become familiar with the necessary routine and functions of a military company, ready and willing to serve when called. The building known as Independence Hall still stands and is located at 715 Main Street.[137]

Boonton's Little Cannon

Probably not as prominent as Summit's "Old Sow" of Revolutionary fame, but equally dear to the hearts of local historians is Boonton's "Little Cannon." Boonton's Little Cannon was made by the men at the Boonton Ironworks. The barrel is about thirty inches long with a bore of two and five-eighths inches, and would be termed a three-pounder. Legend tells us that the barrel was made from Boonton nails melted down for the purpose. This of course was questionable.[138] The

Boonton's Little Cannon.

carriage of the cannon was definitely made at the Ironworks, for the wheels are of the same pattern as the wheels on the hand carts used to move iron and other heavy materials processed at the mill. The carriage parts were hewn from oak, shaped to receive the barrel and fastened together with heavy iron bolts. The letters "B E N" painted on the side of the carriage could very well be the initials of Benjamin Norton who came to Boonton with Philip Wootton and others in 1830, from Staffordshire, England, when the mills were established in the "hollow." It is believed that the cannon was assembled by the men of the Ironworks in the fall of 1860, at the time when the "Wide-Awake" unit was organized.

The cannon was never used as a weapon in combat, but served only as a saluting gun at the mill and to usher in the holidays and celebrations whenever the occasion warranted it. The people of that day were very conscious of our national holidays and the reasons for which they were celebrated, never missing the opportunity to declare themselves and express their feelings. Quoting from the county newspaper, *The Jerseyman*, July 4, 1863, "Fourth of July at Boonton— The day was ushered in by the firing of cannon, ringing of bells, etc." *The Jerseyman*, February 27, 1864, "Washington's Birthday at Boonton—Flags were displayed, bells were rung and a National salute was fired, morning noon and night."

The cannon displayed its purpose again on July 4, 1865, when the men of "Old Pequannoc" were welcomed home from the war. And when the Soldier's Monument, in Boonton, was dedicated on July 4, 1876, honoring the men of Pequannock Township who had fought in the War, Samuel L. Garrison, editor and publisher of the *Boonton Weekly Bulletin*, reported: "At twelve o'clock on Monday night the boom of cannon awakened our citizens and there was little if any sleep after that hour."

Thus the Little Cannon served its purpose, arousing the citizens and helping to express the patriotic fervor that was so ardently displayed in that day. The cannon was used from time to time after that period, and some of the "old timers" recall how the men of the mill would bring out the cannon on a Fourth of July and wake up the Town with their efforts. Finally when the Ironworks was—no more, the Little Cannon disappeared, and the people wondered what became of it.

Boonton had its first door to door mail delivery in 1911, and the late Dawfy B. Righter was appointed one of the first mail carriers. One day, going along his route, which included Plane Street, he went into the dilapidated building that had been the Ironworks office. This building was on the site of the present Bethel A.M.E. Church. His curiosity took him to the sub-cellar, two floors below the street level, and there in the debris he found the cannon. He immediately went across the street to the machine shop of Oscar P. Whitehead and told Mr. Whitehead of his find. With great effort they removed the cannon from its ignominious resting place and carried it to Mr. Whitehead's shop, where it was kept until Mr. Whitehead's retirement in 1933. It was then turned over to the late Oscar P. Myers, who kept it safely in the basement of the Boonton Trust Company. Upon his passing, the cannon was turned over to the writer and restored. For the past several years the Little Cannon has been charged and fired to announce the starting of the Memorial Day observances, again taking up the task it had performed many times in the past, honoring the veterans of all the wars of our country.

Chapter III

Civil War Years
1861–1865

The burdens and responsibilities that became the lot of Abraham Lincoln as our president need not be reviewed. His humility, compassion and reverence were not compatible with the severity and decisiveness that he was obliged to exercise, knowing "if a house be divided against itself, that house cannot stand." Surely his qualifications were not those of a wartime President. On the occasion of his inauguration he delivered a long and thoughtful address, solemnly declaring his fixed purpose to uphold the Constitution, enforce the laws, and preserve the integrity of the Union.

In the early months of '61 the people lived in constant fear of war, being fully aware of the worsening conditions and with full realization that only a miracle could prevent it from happening. Then came the fateful day, April 12, 1861:

> Fire was opened by General Beauregard at 4 A.M., Friday, the 12th, from seven batteries, . . . and at 12:55 P.M. Saturday, the American Flag was lowered, . . . Fort Sumter evacuated by Major Anderson.[139]

Local Patriotic Fervor

The news of this startling event went through the country like wildfire, but the actual shock came with stunning abruptness. The people flocked to the village to gather the news and to comment on the coming conflict. The older men spoke gravely of the deed that was done; the younger men talked of enlisting, none fully realizing the magnitude of things to come.

Three days later, when the President issued his proclamation asking for 75,000 men to defend our national Capitol,[140] the quota of Pequannock Township was promptly filled by volunteers. The response was such that when Governor Charles S. Olden, by proclamation, called for men to make up four regiments in the State, it was accomplished within thirteen days, and men who could not get in because of those regiments being quickly filled, went to nearby States to enlist in regiments there.

Less than one month later, on May 3rd, another call was made for 42,000 men to serve three years, and again the quota of Pequannock Township was oversubscribed. The fervent patriotism of the township knew no bounds, and although quotas were promptly filled, the Company in Boonton was also filled to capacity, the men hoping they could enlist and serve as a unit. The Hon. John Hill had petitioned the Governor to accept this Company, but without success.[141]

A reporter of the *Paterson Guardian*, visiting the Ironworks, found this to say of the activities he saw there:

> The fire of heroism burns brightly in Boonton. The Captain of the military company there had aroused "Old Pequannoc," and at least two hundred of as hardy, stalwart men as ever dashed a bayonet charge, could be raised in a week's time. They were hungering and thirsting after a chance to meet our aristocratic foes. Shall they not have it? The uniformed company is a splendid one, and what a mine of true gold is in the spirit and muscle of the undrilled athletes of that village.

> The Nail Factory now presents an animated appearance. Some two hundred of those savage iron-eating machines have small flags of the stars and stripes pattern affixed to their moving parts, as they keep bobbing up and down in ceaseless movement, help no doubt to fan the flame of love for Country, and for home and honor.

> A subscription paper for a large flag for this particular factory happened to be going around as we visited this department, and a few quarters from our part, brought such a shout from those stentorian throats, as made the noisy rattle

of those hammering monsters of the iron maws like a maiden's whisper in comparison.

Why don't our "City Blues" fraternize with the Boonton and Morristown Companies, and with the remaining Companies at Newark form an independent Company?[142]

The clamor and enthusiasm of these local groups was of such magnitude that it was necessary for Governor Olden to issue a proclamation on the matter so that the people would understand the situation. Herewith is that proclamation:

STATE OF NEW JERSEY
PROCLAMATION BY THE GOVERNOR

Whereas, the Four Regiments called for this State by the President's requisition have been completed, and are in the United States' service;

And whereas, other companies have been organized, and have volunteered their services to the Governor, sufficient to form several additional regiments which I have no authority to accept, as the President has made no further requisition, and I am not advised that any other will be made;

And whereas, it is desirable that the militia of New Jersey generally should be in a state of preparation for any exigency that may arise;

I do, therefore, recommend that all volunteer companies now forming throughout the State and all other persons of the proper age disposed to do so, organize themselves as volunteer companies, according to the act of the Legislature of 1860, as promptly as may be, so that there may be a large body of effective militia in the State, ready for any call that may be made upon them. All volunteer companies thus organized will be armed by the State, with the provisions of the aforesaid act, as soon as proper arms can be obtained.

By the Governor,
CHARLES S. OLDEN.
W. S. Johnson, Secretary of State.
Dated Trenton, May 2, 1861.[143]

A Boy Goes to War

The following is a description of a scene that occurred in a Boonton household early in May, 1861. It was typical of many such incidents, and it is given just as it was written in the "Memoirs" of Charles F. Hopkins, who had the foresight to register his war experiences for posterity.

Among those who had more war spirit than discretion, was a youth of very boyish appearance, yet so full of fight (naturally distances enchanted the view) that he could scarcely take time to eat or sleep—but was more willing to do both later on, when the actual fighting was not as rosily-hued as the dreamed-of-glory to be attained on the battlefield. Quite unwilling to await the seemingly slow process (though found sufficiently swift a few months later) of offering our services and being accepted as a Company; with more patriotic fervor than good sense, on the 3rd of May, 1861, without due parental notice and sanction, I startled the family at the breakfast table (minus the head of the family, who left early to be absent the whole day) with, "Ellen, I want a clean shirt, I am going away!" Ellen, who was my stepmother, and a good one, and her two daughters, who were as sisters, were the only persons present, the one whom I did not wish to consult on the question, my father, was absent as before stated. I had chosen this auspicious time, in order to avoid a collision that might prove all my nicely laid plans abortive. In reply to my good stepmother's question, "Charlie, where are you going?" "To war!" came the prompt reply, and I imagine there may have been some bombast in the tone, for I was chuck full of enthusiasm to go to war. With the tears and pleading of Mother and her daughters, I had to brace up pretty firmly— and won. The bundle was neatly wrapped, and many other things urged upon me, but I was no pack horse then, no matter how much of a pack mule I was later on. I pleaded stage time which was close at hand as I could hear the rumbling of Jake Meslar's thorough-brace, old rocking stage. Hastily embracing and kissing all good-bye, not forgetting to leave a good-bye to the absent father, the stage passed the door—and I became an unexpected passenger.

I sprang to the boot of the old "Ark," crawled to the roof and surprised "Old Jake," who gave me a scowl as I paid him the usual thirty cents for an uncomfortable ride to Denville. To all his inquiries as to where I was going—and believing it none of his business, I was both deaf and dumb. This was the strategy I was practicing, for he may have flanked my position and surrounded me, as he knew I was under age, and had not the consent of my father. These two were great friends, though they differed to the very extreme in politics; but 'tis said that politics make strange bedfellows, which was indeed true in this case . . .

We reached our goal, New York City, and visited the Battery, intending to enlist in the Second Militia Regiment of New York, from which some eight hundred had already gone forward to Washington and the front. When about to enlist, we learned from the newspaper that there had been a mutiny among them at Washington, and thereupon we stoutly refused to become that kind of patriot. We searched from one headquarters to another, until finally, in disgust, we crossed the river to my native State. At Hoboken, I was "taken in" in right smart order, along with another Yankee, whose acquaintance I had made at the Battery, by his proffer to me to share his umbrella. He hailed from the land of the "Wooden Nutmegs," and this friendship was to ripen into a life long comradeship, both in the service and to this hour— with seventy-eight years to my credit, and eighty-five to his. We were sent to Trenton, New Jersey, on the day following our visit to Hoboken, and became members of Company I, First Regiment, New Jersey Volunteers.[144]

A Pole and Flag Raising at Boonton

If ever people had love for their Flag, it was never more in evidence than demonstrated by the affection of our citizens in that day, and flag-raisings always called for a celebration. The flags were large and the poles were high, as one community would try to surpass the others in respect to size. On July 13, 1861, a large pole, one hundred and ten feet high, was raised on the corner of Main and Liberty Streets, near Dr. Grimes' building, which was called "Liberty Hall," and a new flag of great size was flung to the breeze. This was the tenth large pole and flag to be raised in our village besides numerous smaller ones.

A platform was erected on Liberty Street, and George Jenkins, as chairman, introduced other speakers. John Hill, Esq., Rev. G. D. Brewerton, Pastor of the Morristown M.E. Church, Mr. King, of Morristown, and Dr. Grimes were speakers that day. The Washington Cornet Band of Boonton was at its best, and the "Brewerton Zouaves" thrilled the people with their maneuvers. The Brewerton Zouaves were a company of young boys, between the ages of eight and fifteen, organized by Rev. Brewerton, and the discipline and precision displayed attracted the attention of all. Their gay uniforms, consisting of loose fitting pantaloons, short leggin's, a short sleeveless jacket, and a small military cap with a havelock draped from its rear over the neck as a sun-shield, gave these boys a truly military appearance. After the Zouaves finished their drill they marched to their carriages below the hill (Plane Street) and left for home, and thus the ceremony ended.[145]

A Soldier Is Brought Home

The spirit and color that marked the going away of our boys was in vivid contrast to the occasion when a soldier was "brought home." One of the first of these was Samuel McNair. He had enlisted in Captain Southard's Company K, of the First Regiment, New York Engineers, having enlisted in this Company with others from Morris County when the ranks of the New Jersey regiments had been oversubscribed. His military career was brought to an end, when on March 26, 1862, he died, having contracted typhoid fever at Port Royal. His remains were brought to Morristown, and the next morning a procession started its march to Morris Plains, where carriages were waiting to convey the escort consisting of Companies B and C, and the Morris Cornet Band, on their way to Boonton. A brief halt was made at the residence of the father of the deceased, about a mile and half south of Boonton (Old Boonton), where the procession swelled to nearly one hundred carriages, forming a line over a mile and half in length. On the outskirts of Boonton the escort alighted from their wagons and were joined by the Boonton Cornet Band, and with slow and silent tread the long line of mourners wended their way to the Presbyterian Church, where the funeral services were observed. Rev. Daniel Megie preached a short discourse; his text was from Eccl. viii.8: "And there is no discharge from that war." At the close, the procession reformed and Samuel McNair was laid to rest in the cemetery on the hill.[146]

The President's Guard

When the third call for men was made July 24, 1861, Pequannock Township once more contributed generously to the numbers needed, and many men who had served in the first or "three months" call, reenlisted for three years or the duration. Attempts were still being made to have entire companies accepted in New Jersey regiments and when this failed, Captain Duncan of the "Morris Greys" raised a Company for the District of Columbia Volunteers, to be attached to the President's Guard. How proud our citizens must have felt when in The Jerseyman they read the following:

February 1, 1862.
The village of Boonton, in this County, is certainly one of the most patriotic places of its size to be found anywhere in the East. It furnished forty-two members of Captain Duncan's Company, which left Morristown on Tuesday, and

71

has sent altogether, we understand, two hundred-sixty men to war—about one-sixth of its population. Boonton is part of "Old Pequannoc" and she always manages to cover herself with glory.[147]

Charles F. Hopkins

By this time there were some of our men who had distinguished themselves in the war. Most of their brave acts have passed unnoticed and unrecorded; but fortunate are we, indeed, when we are able to read first hand, the account of one such act, entered in the "Memoirs" of Charles F. Hopkins. We salute Charles F. Hopkins, first, for his bravery in the war; and second, for his foresight, allowing the future generations of his family and community to thrill to the record of his deeds. His description of the event follows:

A charge came suddenly, out of the northwest—the flying columns of Stonewall Jackson, whose unique name was attached at First Bull Run, and now was again to add laurels to his fame by an attempt to flank our right wing, compelling us to fall back to Gaines Mills, and later to Gaines Hills, near the home of Dr. William Gaines, where on June 27, 1862, the unlucky Friday, so called, we engaged the enemy in a hotly contested fight, in which the writer was twice flesh wounded, and while falling back, found Sergeant Richard A. Donnelly, of my Company, and my close friend, badly wounded with a shattered leg. He wanted to be taken from the field of carnage, then raging like a holocaust of Hell, and the chances were as one in a thousand that both of us would reach cover. I would not refuse my friend Dick in such a case, and under the terrific, galling cross fire, carried him to a supposed place of safety into the hands of comrades of our Company—though he was made prisoner later on—and afterward recovering from the temporary blindness and exhaustion due to a 1200 yard dash with a load of no mean proportions, as my comrade was over six feet and I was only five feet nine, I again took to fighting, and after about twenty

MEDAL OF HONOR CERTIFICATE

ISSUED UNDER THE PROVISIONS OF THE ACT OF CONGRESS APPROVED APRIL 27, 1916.

To whom it may concern:

This is to Certify, That *Charles F. Hopkins* was *enrolled* on the *tenth* day of *June*, 1861, to serve *three years*, and was discharged on the *twenty-first* day of *April*, 1865, by reason of *being a paroled prisoner of war* while holding the grade of *Private*, in Company *I First* Regiment of *New Jersey Infantry Volunteers*; that a medal of honor was awarded to him on the *second* day of *July*, 1892, for *distinguished conduct in action at the battle of Gaines Mills, Va. June 27, 1862, when he voluntarily carried a wounded comrade under heavy fire, to a place of safety: and though twice wounded in the act he continued in action until again severely wounded,* that his name was entered and recorded on the Army and Navy Medal of Honor Roll on the *second* day of *June*, 1916, as authorized under the provisions of the Act of Congress approved April 27, 1916, and that he is entitled to receive the special pension granted by that Act.

Given at the War Department, Washington, D. C., this *fourth* day of *October*, 1916.

By authority of the Secretary of War:

H. P. McCain
The Adjutant General.

Form No. 588—A.G.O.
Ed. May 1-16—600.

240853!

C.F.H. died 2/1932

Medal of Honor Certificate of Charles F. Hopkins.

minutes was shot in the left side of the head. To all appearances, my comrades said, I must be dead, and they passed on in that belief, and reported me "dead on the field of battle." I slowly came back to this world as, during the shock, I had passed into strange places as well as having a vivid panorama of my whole past life in that short time of not over ten minutes. While it was not all virtue, I had not much to deeply blush for, perhaps because I had not lived very long and was country bred. I managed to struggle to my feet and attempted to make my way to where our men had formed a line to stay the onrush of the elated enemy, and was almost run down by the charge of Rush's Lancers, who swiftly came on to meet the advancing enemy; and but for the quick thought of the left guide of the Squadron, I would have been trampled to death beneath the feet of the close column of horses. Reaching the line of battle, I was passed to the rear; taken to the field hospital, which was near Woodbury or Engineer's Ridge and placed under the low hanging branches of an apple tree to wait my turn for surgical treatment, which came about two o'clock in the morning. A ball and two buck shot were removed from the wounded head and neck. They placed the "ball and buck" in my pocket and returned me to the shelter of the tree to die from bleeding or saved by Nature's choice.[148]

On July 2, 1892, Charles F. Hopkins was awarded the Congressional Medal of Honor. Although belated in its presentation, the Medal of Honor Certificate bears witness to his brave deed.[149]

More Volunteers

President Lincoln issued another call for three hundred thousand volunteers on July 7, 1862,[150] and again Pequannock Township fell to the task of filling its quota. The older citizens held meetings to help stimulate the enlistment of our men, and at a meeting held here on July 28th, a large and enthusiastic crowd heard speeches by John Hill and others. Resolutions were passed, among them one to raise one thousand dollars for bounty money to be paid volunteers who enlisted from "Old Pequannock." [151]

Our townsman, John Hill, deserving all that was ever said and done in his honor, was truly a remarkable citizen. His

74

personal sacrifices, given willingly to serve the Cause, earned for him the respect of everyone. He worked hard, going about the Township encouraging the boys to enlist, helping those who had problems, giving counsel where it was needed; in all he was looked upon as a leader in the community. He was proud of our record, and would not tolerate its being misquoted. This was demonstrated when in publishing the lists of enlistments and deficiencies for the County, one of the editors made the grave error of not giving the true figures for Pequannock Township. Mr. Hill took the editor to task in no uncertain manner. The following is a portion of Mr. Hill's letter:

Boonton, September 1, 1862.

Mr. Editor:

Dear Sir:

I see in your paper of Saturday last, reference made to an article in the "Sussex Herald" of last week, stating that Pequannoc Township had failed to furnish her portion of Volunteers to the war. It certainly shows great ignorance on the part of the Editor of that paper. He probably made that assertion from the large number of men called for in her quota to furnish in the last call for nine-months men; and if the inference was got from that, he is inexcusable, for I hold that no Editor has a right to belie any person or persons, or make false statements in relation to townships or counties, unless he first informs himself of the facts.

But few townships in the State have been more patriotic, shown stronger attachment to the Union, sent forth her men sooner, and answered every call of the Government quicker, than this Township. She was among the first to volunteer a full, well-drilled Company to the Governor of the State, first for three months, in answer to the first call, and then for three years in answer to the second call, which offer I made in person, and each time refused. Our men then scattered and joined different companies in and out of the State. Over fifty men have enlisted in the Army from the Nail Factory, and a large number from other parts of the Works. It has been with difficulty at times the Ironworks could keep running on account of so many men enlisting in the Army to go to War, and men too who were earning, some of them, double and triple the amount paid by the Government in regular pay, bounties, etc.

Previous to the call for nine-months men this Township furnished and sent out, as recorded on the Commissioner's Roll, 260, and a large number from the middle of the Township, the names not yet returned, which I think will be no less than twenty. There were in the President's Guard from this Town last winter, thirty-eight, and on Monday last we sent 127, making a total of 445, and if the names of all who have gone could be got, I have no doubt it would reach 450, nearly one-half of the whole vote of the Township, which in 1860 was 1040. If there is any township in the State that has done better I should like to know where it is . . .

I think I speak the voice of the citizens of this Town when I say that we are all, Democrats and Republicans, firm for the Union, the Constitution and the good old Flag of our fathers, and ready and willing to furnish all the men the Government may call for from this Town to give them help to save the Country, and continue to us those blessings we have enjoyed under the Constitution of the United States.

Respectfully yours,
John Hill.[152]

When the men of Pequannock left for the War, they had no doubts in their hearts and minds that their sacrifice and service was appreciated to the fullest degree. Their leaving was an event to be remembered, as reported in *The Jerseyman*:

Morristown was a blaze of excitement on Monday last, caused by the arrival of the Volunteers from Pequannoc Township. They came in wagons, accompanied by their Fathers, Mothers, sons, brothers and sisters, headed by the

Boonton Band, and marshalled by their patriotic fellow-citizen, John Hill, Esq. The number of wagons is said to have exceeded a hundred and fifty, and as they marched through the Town, with music playing and flags flying, they presented an imposing appearance, and attracted great attention. After partaking of refreshments at Washington Hall, the Volunteers left for Newark in the afternoon train.[153]

These men were the first to be accepted as a group, and were known as the Pequannoc Company, all having come from this Township. Their first destination was Camp Frelinghuysen, near Newark, and a delegation from our town visited them on their first Saturday in camp. At this time John Hill, acting as spokesman for the delegation, presented to Captain James Plant, a sword and pistol; and to First Lieutenant George W. Esten, a sword; the swords and pistol being gifts from the citizens of Boonton. Second Lieutenant George Anthony was presented with a sword, the gift of his fellow-workmen in the Nail Factory.[154]

When these men completed their initial training at Camp Frelinghuysen the Company was broken up to fill the gaps caused by losses in the field, and their military careers carried them in many directions. As one walks among the graves in the cemeteries of Boonton and neighboring places, the names of many of those men can be found on the headstones, with only brief reference made to the Company and Regiment in which they served, offering mute and inadequate testimony to the greatness of their deeds.

The Union League

The citizens at home were serious and dedicated in their activities and support of the Northern Cause, and in the spring of 1863, Union Leagues were formed, Boonton having an organization of more than two hundred members. The officers were

John Hill, President; George Jenkins, Vice President; O. F. Gaines, Secretary; and Joseph Milner, Treasurer. The Executive Committee members were William Lathrop, George W. Esten, John L. Kanouse, G. V. S. Rickards, John Grimes, E. E. Willis, John Jaques, William Phillips, Isaac H. Kingsland, Amzi Burroughs and N. T. Jennings.

The purpose of the Union League at Boonton was defined in its By-Laws; a portion follows:

> The Association is organized under the Pledge of The Loyal National League.
> We, the undersigned, citizens of the United States, hereby associate ourselves under the name and title of the Union League of Boonton.
> We pledge ourselves to an unconditional loyalty to the Government of the United States, to an unwavering support of its efforts to suppress the Rebellion, and to spare no endeavor to maintain unimpaired the National unity, both in principle and territorial boundary.
> The primary object of this League is, and shall be, to bind together all loyal men, of all trades and professions, in a common union to maintain the power, glory and integrity of the North.
> All persons signing this pledge shall be members of the Union League of Boonton . . . . [155]

Day of National Prayer

While we were asking men to bind themselves in a common union to "maintain the power, glory and integrity of the North," it must have come as a shock to our people when President Lincoln reminded them that we, "Intoxicated with unbroken success, have become too self-sufficient to feel the necessity of redeeming grace, too proud to pray to the God that made us."

On the 30th of March, 1863, President Lincoln issued a proclamation for a day of National Prayer and Humiliation.[156] I will not attempt to shorten it; to paraphrase would be presumptuous, and would detract from its significance.

A Proclamation by the President of the United States of America

Whereas, the Senate of the United States devotedly recognizing the supreme authority and government of Almighty God in all affairs of men of nations, has, by a resolution requested the President to designate and set apart a day for National Prayer and Humiliation, and,

Whereas, It is the duty of nations, as well as of men, to own their dependence upon the overruling power of God, to confess their sins and transgressions, in humble sorrow, yet with the assured hope that genuine repentance will lead to mercy and pardon, and to recognize the sublime truths announced in the Holy Scriptures and proven by all history, that those nations only are blessed whose God is the Lord:

And inasmuch as we know that, by His Divine Law, nations like individuals, are subjected to punishment and chastisement in this world, may we not justly fear that the awful calamity of civil war which now so desolates the land, may be but a punishment inflicted upon us for our presumptuous sins, to the needful end of our national reformation as a whole People? We have been the recipients of the choicest bounties of Heaven. We have been preserved, these many years, in peace and prosperity. We have grown in numbers, wealth, and power as no other nation has ever grown. But we have forgotten God. We have forgotten the gracious hand which preserved us in peace, and multiplied and enriched and strengthened us; and we have vainly imagined, in the deceitfulness of our hearts, that all these were produced by some superior wisdom of our own. Intoxicated with unbroken success, we have become too self-sufficient to feel the necessity of redeeming and preserving grace, too proud to pray to the God that made us.

It behooves us, then, to humble ourselves before the offended Power, to confess our national sins, and pray for clemency and forgiveness.

Now, therefore, in compliance with the request, and fully concurring in the views of the Senate, I do by this my proclamation designate and set apart Thursday, the 30th day of April, 1863, as a day of national humiliation, fasting and prayer. And I do hereby request that all the people to abstain on that day from their ordinary secular pursuits, and to unite, at their several places of public worship and respective homes, in keeping the day holy to the Lord, and devoted to the humble discharge of the religious duties proper to that solemn occasion.

All this being done, in sincerity and truth, let us then rest humbly in the hope, authorized by the Divine Teachings, that the united cry of the Nation will be heard on High, and answered with blessings, no less than the pardon of our national sins, and restoration of our now divided country to its former happy condition of unity and peace.

In witness whereof, I have hereunto set my hand, and caused the Seal of the United States to be affixed.

Done at the City of Washington, this thirtieth day of March, in the year of our Lord, one thousand eight hundred and sixty-three, and the independence of the United States the eighty-seventh.

ABRAHAM LINCOLN

(L.S.)
By the President:
William H. Seward,
Secretary of State.

Wartime Prosperity

The war was revealing its effects here at home in the nature of increased prosperity. The Ironworks was operating to its greatest capacity; the men were earning wages better than average, and as previously stated, the payroll at the mill exceeded $30,000 per month.[157] Many of the workers took advantage of this steady flow of money and purchased lots

PRICES PAID

FOR

MAKING NAILS

AT BOONTON, NEW JERSEY, 1867.

SPIKES.

3 inch	$22\frac{1}{2}$
$3\frac{1}{2}$ "	$22\frac{1}{2}$
4 "	$18\frac{3}{4}$
$4\frac{1}{2}$ "	$18\frac{3}{4}$
5 "	$17\frac{1}{2}$
$5\frac{1}{2}$ "	$17\frac{1}{2}$
6 "	$17\frac{1}{2}$
$6\frac{1}{2}$ "	$17\frac{1}{2}$
7 "	$17\frac{1}{2}$
8 "	$17\frac{1}{2}$

NAILS.

2d		1.87\frac{1}{2}$
3d	(fine)	2.06
3d	(common)	1.40
4d		$93\frac{3}{4}$
5d		75
6d		$62\frac{1}{2}$
7d		50
8d		$38\frac{3}{4}$
9d		35
10d		30
12d		$26\frac{1}{4}$
20d		$23\frac{3}{4}$
30d		$22\frac{1}{2}$
40d		$21\frac{1}{4}$
50d		$18\frac{3}{4}$
60d		$17\frac{1}{2}$

TRUNK NAILS.

4d	$1.40
5d	1.12$\frac{1}{2}$

CAR NAILS.

10d	$28\frac{3}{4}$
12d	$26\frac{1}{4}$

FINISHING NAILS.

4d	$1.40
5d	1.12$\frac{1}{2}$
6d	$87\frac{1}{2}$

Finishing Nails Continued.

8d	57
10d	$37\frac{3}{4}$
12d	30

COOPER NAILS.

3d	Slate 140	$1.40
4d	Slate 93¾	$93\frac{3}{4}$
5d	Slate 77/10	75
6d		62
8d		$38\frac{3}{4}$
10d		30

FLOOR NAILS.

6d	$62\frac{1}{2}$
8d	$41\frac{1}{4}$
10d	30
12d	$26\frac{1}{4}$

FENCE NAILS.

6d	50
7d	40
8d	30
10d	$26\frac{1}{4}$
12d	$23\frac{3}{4}$
20d	$22\frac{1}{2}$

BOX NAILS.

5d	1.12\frac{1}{2}$
6d	$87\frac{1}{2}$
8d	57
10d	$38\frac{3}{4}$

CLINCH NAILS.

2 inch	70
$2\frac{1}{4}$ "	62
$2\frac{1}{2}$ "	$48\frac{3}{4}$
$2\frac{3}{4}$ "	$43\frac{3}{4}$
3 "	$37\frac{1}{4}$
$3\frac{1}{4}$ "	$33\frac{3}{4}$
$3\frac{1}{2}$ "	$31\frac{1}{4}$
4 "	$28\frac{1}{4}$

AMZI PIERSON, Printer, 140 Market Street, Newark, N. J.

Nail price list.

from the mill owners, and later built their homes up on the hillside. Some, with an aptitude for increasing their fortunes, invested in property and acquired considerable holdings. If one were to compare the Hughes Map of Boonton, 1857, with the Beers Map of Boonton, 1868, it would reveal the foregoing to be true.

The Morris Canal in 1863 had its best year since its inception. The total revenue for the year was reported at over $300,000; and it was said that two-thirds of the materials and produce transported in the boats going East, were unloaded at Boonton.[158]

J. C. Lord, of Fuller & Lord, the owners of the Ironworks, was also a director of the Morris and Essex Railroad. He was exerting his influence to have a branch of the railroad constructed from Denville to Boonton, to replace the stage line in use at that time; and also to furnish a faster means of transportation to supply the mill with its needs and to deliver the finished products to points not accessible via the canal route. This spur between Denville and Boonton was completed and placed in operation in 1867.[159]

Martin Shaw had charge of the nail shipments that were taken from the large storehouse and loaded on the canal boats. In the "Shipping Book" of Martin Shaw is an entry on Thursday, October 3, 1867. In the margin, in red ink, is the notation, "First nails shipped by M & E R.R. from Boonton." The nails shipped that week totalled 5,181 kegs.[160]

Income Tax

It is interesting to note, along with these items describing the prosperity of that era, that the citizens were subject to an income tax. The collectors of internal revenue issued notices to persons whose income warranted the payment of the tax, and it was payable every six months. The tax due was three per cent on all incomes over $600, after deducting from the excess the amount of rent actually paid by the person. Later, in 1865, a special war tax of five per cent was assessed based on the 1863 incomes. The largest amount of tax paid by a person was $1,118; the smallest amount was 90 cents. These were listed in the report of Hanover and Pequannock Townships.[161]

"Politics" Again

In reference to the unity of the people and their reactions to both national and local issues, there were exceptions in both parties, and their remarks and behavior reflected their feelings, especially at election time. If a person wanted to give vent to his feelings, the common thing to do was to write to the paper of his choice so that his views would be published in a manner satisfactory to him, and as a result, assertions and denials ran rampant. In the local election contests in the Spring of 1863, one of the candidates, who was termed a "Copperhead" by his opponents, made the accusation that the "Boontonists" were "owned" by the Ironworks, and that they had resorted to running their wagons to and fro from the polls in all directions, causing his defeat. In answer to this, the opposing candidate stated that, "The Boontonists no doubt are those that are loyal to their Country, the Government and their honor, and as to the contemptible insinuation that the Boontonists were 'owned' by the Ironworks, this was an indication of a sorely defeated rebel sympathizer, and the election proved the voters of 'Old Pequannoc' would not tolerate his kind." [162]

In another instance one of the department heads at the mill had spoken in vehement denunciation of President Lincoln's policies. The men who heard him, not being able to find words to suit the occasion, took hold of him and escorted him to the large fountain in the center of the mill, where they dunked him again and again until he "took back" the remarks he had made so all could hear, and extracted from him a promise that he would not repeat them again. Freedom of speech had its bad moments in Boonton.[163]

Boonton's Volunteer Companies

The Fourth of July celebration in 1863 was observed with the customary firing of cannon, ringing of bells, a large parade and concluded with a grand display of fireworks. The proceeds of the celebration were given to the Sanitary Commission (a counterpart of our Red Cross today) for the benefit of the sick and wounded soldiers. Included in the parade were the men from all the departments of the Ironworks, over five hundred strong; but the main attraction was the drilling of Company G, under Captain James Plant. This Company bad in its ranks many men from Pequannock Township and was the Company that was organized here in September, 1862.[164]

It would be quite impossible to follow the entire activities of Captain Plant and his Company. His service record states that he was honorably discharged, July 2, 1863.[165] The Company was drawn upon to make replacements in other companies and new men were taken in to fill the ranks. In August of 1863 we find two companies in Boonton, Company G and H of the First Regiment.[166] The officers of these companies were elected before Col. Runyan of the First Regiment. The officers of Company C were Captain Edwin Bishop, First Lieutenant Daniel Dillon and Second Lieutenant Jacob L. Hutt. The officers of Company H were Captain Richard Foster, First Lieutenant George Carlough, and Second Lieutenant William Milner. All of those mentioned had previously served and reenlisted; their experience was of great help to these temporary companies.

Pequannock Township was known for offering the most liberal inducements to volunteers in its efforts to fill the ranks of her new companies. Meetings were held for this purpose and pledges were made by the citizens to furnish bounty money paid to the volunteers. Notices were placed in the County newspapers and bold-face type would proclaim that "PEQUANNOC TOWNSHIP WANTS 133 VOLUN-TEERS, and Will Pay Three Hundred and Sixty Dollars

Bounty." Then would follow a lengthy description of the advantages and pay one would receive in the Army, including provisions, clothing, medical attention, etc. This particular notice was signed by John Hill, John L. Kanouse, John Grimes, Sam'l VanNess and Stephen Post.[167]

The Committee must have done their work well, for a news item of January 23, 1864, noted the following:

> It will prove a source of pride and gratification to all who feel an interest in "Old Pequannoc" to learn that she has filled her quota of 133 men under the recent calls—being the only township in the County which has done so, and at most the only one that has attempted to do anything in that direction. This glorious old Township is loyal to the core, and always foremost in every good work. Let her have the honor that is her due.[168]

Following the completion of this call the men from Pequannock were assigned to Company K, First Regiment, New Jersey Volunteers, and a new complement of officers were selected and commissioned. Richard Foster was named Captain of Company K, and held that command for the remainder of his army career.

The forming of Company K, in Boonton, was followed by a notable occasion for our Town. The following is the account as it was published in *The Jerseyman*:

Sword Presentation at Boonton,
to the Officers of Company K,
New Jersey Volunteers.

Boonton, January 26, 1864.

Saturday evening last was an occasion of no little interest to the citizens of our village. Pequannoc Township having filled her quota, and obtained permission to form a Company from the Town, to be attached to the First Regiment, now in the field, and the officers had been commissioned, and were presented with their commissions and their swords in the presence of a large audience, convened for the occasion—the presentation being made by the Hon. John Hill. Captain Richard Foster having already been presented with a beautiful sword and belt by his men in camp, it was exhibited to the delight of all present; and the Captain was presented with a silk sash and pistol by his friends of the Town. First Lieutenant William Miers was presented with a handsome sword, belt and sash, coming from his fellow workmen in the Rolling Mill, and also a pistol from Mr. Thomas Bickley. Second Lieutenant William Milner was also the recipient of a beautiful sword, belt and sash from his fellow workmen in the Plate Mill, and Jacob L. Hutt, First Sergeant, was presented with a pistol by the members of the Arcana Lodge No. 60. Captain Foster replied to the presentation by an enthusiastic speech, pledging himself and his Company to maintain the honor of the Township, and that the confidence reposed in him should not be misplaced.

The presentations were interspersed with music by the Washington Cornet Band, and the cheers from the loyal audience assembled. Win. C. Lathrop, Esq., also made a stirring and patriotic speech. The occasion was one of great interest and enthusiasm.

This is the second full Company this Township has sent to the war, and makes 545 men sent since the war broke out, from a population of 6,000, and a voting population of 1,100; and there are more left, anxious to go forth to defend our glorious Union, and the good Old Flag of our Fathers; her sons of the present age are not unlike those of '76, when, as the records of the Township show, 177 true, loyal and patriotic men volunteered for the defense of our liberties, and for the right.

The citizens of "Old Pequannoc" take this opportunity to return their warmest thanks to the Governor of the State, Adjutant-General Stockton, and Quarter-Master-General Perrine, for the aid and assistance rendered in getting up and organizing Company K. May the State always be governed by officers as faithful, loyal and patriotic.[169]

Less than one week after the honoring of Captain Foster and his officers, another draft was announced, February 1, 1864, calling for five hundred thousand men by the 10th of March;[170] and on March 14, 1864, an additional two hundred thousand men were called;[171] the 15th of April being designated as the day when drafts would be made to complete the quotas.

The lack of sufficient time for public meetings and demonstrations created a problem to the committee that was urging the men to volunteer, and it was necessary to resort to private, personal calls to make the contact with the eligibles. Little hope was held for success, and it was feared our cherished record was at its end. The deficiency for Morris County was 795 men, and of this number Pequannoc's share was 79 men.[172] Fortunately, there were several delays, and the date for the drawing was set ahead with each delay, until it was finally announced that Monday, May 29th, the draft would be made to fill the deficiencies. In the meantime the committee, led by John Hill, was making every effort possible to fill our quota before that day. The day arrived, and at Washington Hall, in Morristown, the drawing of the names commenced. The drawing was done by townships, and before Pequannock was called, Major Brown, who was in charge of the draft in Morristown, received a telegram from Col. Buchanan, of Newark, directing him to postpone the draft of Pequannock for the present, it being understood that the quota for that Township had been filled.[173] John Hill and his committee had succeeded again.

"Old Pequannock" had upheld her enviable record; at no time was a man drafted in this Township, and it is believed that it was the only township in the entire State that could claim that distinction. John Hill had given many hours of his time, making speeches and contacting the men personally, and it was largely through his efforts that this honor was ours to hold. In recognition of this great service, and in appreciation of his efforts, the citizens of Pequannock raised a purse of money which a committee presented to Mr. Hill. Mr. Hill wrote a letter of thanks to that committee.[174] and this letter came into the author's hands a number of years ago. It reads as follows:

Boonton, June 21, 1864.

Messrs., N. A. Myers, George Anthony, John Myers and others,

Gentlemen,

On my return home Saturday evening, I found your letter congratulating me on having succeeded in filling the Quota of this Township.

The kind feelings expressed therein, was very gratifying to me, and would have been sufficient for my warmest thanks, and kind remembrance of you all—but when I found enclosed the handsome sum of One Hundred and Seventy Dollars, as a further testimonial of your good feeling, and appreciation, of my services, to relieve the Township of a draft, I felt not a little nonplussed, so unexpected, and unlooked for testimonial, and did it not come from the source, and manner it has, I could not consent to receive it, for I feel in what I have done, it is no more than a duty, I owe the Township and our Country, though I have for a long time been deprived of the comforts of home and have given my time and suffered pecuniary loss, yet it has been done cheerfully, without expectation of reward, or pay, for the same. It would have been enough for me to know, in the spirit of your letter, that my services had met the approbation and satisfaction of my neighbors and fellow Townsmen, and more than repaid me for all privations, care and labor endured.

Therefore feeling as you say that your gift is "Cheerfully and willingly presented, not for value, but gratitude and respect for you," I accept it and return to you my heartfelt thanks for the same. Hoping the time may come when the War shall be brought to a close, no more calls be made for men, and Peace shall be proclaimed throughout the land,— And that Heaven's richest blessings may rest upon you all is my humble prayer —

I am truly your friend and fellow citizen,
JOHN HILL.

When one pauses to think about John Hill's activities, it is difficult to perceive how anyone could resign oneself to the far-reaching scope of the situations that commanded his attention. At short notice he would attend and be the principal speaker at a patriotic gathering, and his words would encourage and fan the spark of patriotism in our people. We have already told of his part as chairman of the committee that found the men to fill our quotas and also solicited the necessary funds to help the families of these men. His dedication and service to his fellow-man was indeed the result of his early Christian training. This was exemplified in the service he gave to our men in the camps and hospitals in and about Washington. There he spent many hours with the men, taking care of their intimate needs and doing everything possible to help and make things easier for the men and their families.[175]

Captain Foster's Company

The men of Captain Foster's Company had their first harsh experiences at the "Wilderness," May 5-7, and John Hill sent home the first list of casualties of that Company.[176] He gave the losses as follows:

Killed—George Crawford, Boonton; Thomas Davis, Boonton; James Crane, White Hall [Towaco]; James W. Howell, Mendham.

Missing—Richard Vincent, Boonton; Patrick Carey, Boonton.

Wounded—John E. Cook, hand, Boonton; B. Riley, hand, Boonton; Thomas Ryan, hand, Boonton; William Jones, arm, Boonton; John Peer, leg, Boonton; George Nix, leg, Boonton; William A. Wright, hand, Stoney Brook; John Meager, hand, Newark; Patrick Haley, leg, Mendham; N. Teets, hand, West Milford, Pa.

It was later revealed that Richard Vincent, who had been reported missing, had been wounded and captured, and sent to Andersonville prison, where he died.

Captain Foster's command of Company K was brought to an end when at Spottsylvania Court House he was wounded and later died of the effects of the wound. John Hill was with Captain Foster when he died. The notice of his death, as it was published in *The Jerseyman*,[177] was received with great sorrow by our citizens. Herewith is that notice:

Captain Richard Foster, when the War broke out in May 1861, enlisted as a private in Company H, Second Regiment, New Jersey Volunteers, in command of Edwin Bishop. He proved a good soldier; was in the seven days' battle before Richmond in 1862, and was severely wounded, taken prisoner, carried to Richmond, placed in Libby Prison, after a while paroled, finally exchanged, and in October 1862 discharged on account of his wounds. In December last, an effort was made to raise the quota of Pequannoc Township, and he volunteered to raise a Company, and with the assistance of some of the citizens of the township, succeeded. He was commissioned Captain of the Company, and in February joined the Twelfth Regiment, having a full Company of 103 men. We have been told he made a good soldier, and in battle brave and faithful. His Company, urged on by his courage and bravery, fought well. He was wounded in the knee on the 12th of May, at Spottsylvania Court House, while leading his Command in their fearful charge on the enemy's breastworks. He suffered much for want of care in the Fredericksburg hospital. On the 25th he arrived in Washington, and on the 27th the wounded leg was amputated above the knee, since which time he continued to fail, till death terminated his sufferings on Tuesday, the 14th inst. He remarked a few days before his death, "In whatever way this may end, I have tried to do my duty. No men fought better than those of my Company. I am sorry I have lost my leg; if it had been an arm I could go back to my Company; I don't like to leave the boys." Few men have proved themselves more brave, patriotic and self-sacrificing than Captain Foster. He was forty years of age.

Captain Foster was typical of many men who served and died for their Country, and as years go by the stories of their brave acts pass into oblivion, unless by chance they are brought to light in this or some similar manner. Surely they deserve a memorial commensurate to their deeds.

Deserters—None from Pequannock Township

Notices were placed in the newspapers by the Provost Marshal of the State offering thirty dollars reward for the arrest and delivery of a deserter, and a warning was issued to the citizens that a fine of five hundred dollars would be imposed for the aiding, harboring or employing persons wanted for desertion. Complete lists were published giving the deserter's name, address, age and occupation, and these lists were given to the townships. These were men who failed to answer when notified to report for duty and were therefore considered deserters. One of the lists published contained 323 names of Morris County men who had so defected. Of the eleven townships in Morris County, the Townships of Pequannock and Chatham were conspicuous by their absence among those mentioned.[178]

The Call for Men Ends

About six months had passed since the task of filling our quota in the last call was accomplished. President Lincoln issued another call for three hundred thousand men to make up the deficiencies throughout the States of the North.[179] Also, Governor Joel Parker of New Jersey had issued a proclamation in which he told of our reverses in Maryland and that our National Capitol was seriously threatened. He stated that although New Jersey had not been officially called upon for troops in this emergency, he regarded the danger imminent. He called upon the citizens of the State to organize immediately and to report to the Adjutant General of the State for thirty days service in Pennsylvania, Maryland and the District of Columbia. This order naturally created great excitement, but it was not carried out.[180]

In the last call for five hundred thousand men, New Jersey's assignment was 15,891; of this number the allotment to Morris County was 655 and Pequannock's share was 115 men. Again in December of 1864 a call was made for three hundred thousand men, and of this call Pequannock was asked to furnish 76 men. It seemed that the demands would never end, but before these calls were consummated the War had taken a favorable turn, and several days after the surrender of General Lee, April 9, 1865, it was announced that the draft and recruiting had come to an end.[181]

End of the War—The Assassination of President Lincoln

The pronouncement of the War's end, the assassination of President Lincoln, and the few days that elapsed until he was laid to rest, all occurred within the span of eleven days. Considering the imposing position these occurrences occupy in our history, they should not pass without comment. It is strange indeed that nothing could be found to tell us how our townspeople received the news, or how they reacted. Lengthy items describing the receiving of the news and details of the observance by the citizens of other places were found in the newspapers of the County, and from the accounts given, we may assume that the reaction and observance was similar in Boonton.

With the knowledge of the dedicated participation of our people in the cause of the Union, and the loyalty and respect shown President Lincoln by the great majority of our citizens, it is not difficult to conceive and visualize the consequent display of emotion that followed the receiving of the reports. The welcome news of the War's end, with its resultant jubilation, was placed in vivid contrast to the overwhelming sorrow that followed the announcement of the assassination of our President. *The Jerseyman* gave the following reports:

PEACE THROUGH VICTORY!
THE REBELLION CRUSHED!
Gen. Lee Surrenders With
His Whole Army.

Sunday, the 9th of April, was made ever memorial in the glorious history of the Nation, by the announcement of the SURRENDER OF GEN. LEE AND HIS WHOLE ARMY. It is the harbinger of an immediate and glorious Peace, a Peace gloriously won by the grand courage, and unshaken faith in their cause of the splendid Armies of the Potomac and the James, aided by their glory-crowned brethren under Sherman and Sheridan and Thomas and Hancock, and the heroes of the ocean who have kept watch and ward along our coasts from the Delaware to the Rio Grande. It is the end of the Confederacy. And as nothing can tell the story as well as the official correspondence, we give it entire:

WAR DEPARTMENT, WASHINGTON
April 9, 1865, 9 o'clock P.M.
To Maj.-Gen. Dix:

This Department has received the official report of the surrender of Gen. Lee and his army to Lieut.-Gen. Grant on the terms proposed by Gen. Grant. Details will be given as speedily as possible.

Edwin M. Stanton,
Secretary of War.

HDQTRS. ARMIES OF THE UNITED STATES
April 9, 1865, 4:30 P.M.

Hon. Edwin M. Stanton, Secretary of War:
Gen. Lee surrendered the army of Northern Virginia this afternoon upon the terms proposed by myself. The accompanying correspondence will show the conditions fully.

U. S. Grant, Lieut.-Gen.

Then followed the expected display of protocol by the exchange of numerous communications between Lieutenant General Ulysses S. Grant and General Robert E. Lee, thereby consummating the surrender of General Lee.[182]

And, from *The Jerseyman* of April 22, 1865:[183]

PRESIDENT LINCOLN ASSASSINATED.
ATTEMPT TO MURDER SEC'Y SEWARD.

The great joy of our victories, so promising in view of peace, has been abruptly broken and supplanted with a sorrow as great, by an event that no true American ever believed possible in this country. President Lincoln has been assassinated by a hand raised in behalf of these traitors, whose quarter of a century of plotting thus receives its appropriate stamp just as their hollow hopes are bursting into ruin.

The time selected was in many respects opportune for the commission of the terrible act. It had been widely published that the President, and General Grant, with their wives and others, were to be present at the performance at Ford's Theatre on Friday evening, April 14th. Mr. Colfax, Speaker of the House of Representatives, called at the White House in the evening, and Mr. Lincoln remarked that he did not want to go, especially as Mrs. Lincoln was not well, but as General Grant had been obliged to go North, he was unwilling further to disappoint the people. He went, and occupied a box in a tier above the stage, together with his wife, another lady, and an officer of the, army. During a momentary hush, while an actor was preparing to enter upon the stage, the report of a pistol was heard, but without exciting suspicion in the unsuspecting audience. But loud screams were heard from Mrs. Lincoln, and at the same instant a man was seen to leap from the box down to the stage, brandishing a large dagger, and shouting "Sic semper tyrannis!" (the motto of the State of Virginia) and "The South is avenged!" He rushed across the stage, and out of the side door . . .

The flags that had been so proudly displayed were lowered to half-mast as a Nation went into mourning, and the draping of the churches, the places of business and the homes began to reflect the sorrow that was felt. Was this "but a punishment inflicted upon us for our presumptuous sins, to the needful end of our reformation as a whole people?" (President Lincoln's proclamation March 30, 1863). Surely his untimely death contributed more than any other single factor in accomplishing President Lincoln's most fervent wish—"our reformation as a whole people."

Sunday was given to special services that spoke of our great loss, and on Monday some of our citizens journeyed to Newark to witness the train carrying the President, as it moved slowly through the vast crowd of people assembled there.

On Wednesday, the day of the funeral, the Ironworks and all places of business closed for the day. Services were held at the Presbyterian Church at noon. The church was filled to capacity, people standing in the rear and a large number stood outside, unable to enter the doors. The Rev. Daniel E. Megie preached an impressive sermon, long to be remembered by those who listened. Services were again held in the evening, at which time Rev. Megie offered prayers and appropriate hymns were sung, as the people joined in a last farewell to President Lincoln.

Chapter IV

Post-War Years

"Welcome Home"—July 4th, 1865

The sorrow and bereavement that followed President Lincoln's death left a wound in the hearts of the people that was slow to heal; but with the War at an end, and the men returned to their homes, plans were made for a "Welcome Home" celebration. What better day could they have chosen than the Fourth of July? In our generation we have witnessed the welcoming of our men who returned victorious from two major wars, and in each instance we felt the celebration befitting the occasion. But, after reviewing the accounts given of the Fourth of July, 1865, one might conclude our generation could have done better. Perhaps the people were more demonstrative in that day, unafraid to let others witness their emotions, always generous in their participation in affairs of their community, and humbly grateful to those who gave all or a portion of their lives that we might continue as a united people. Herewith is the account of that celebration as it was published in *The Jerseyman*, July 15, 1865:

> The Fourth of July was celebrated in "Old Pequannoc" at Boonton, in a manner worthy of the occasion. The citizens from all parts of the Township joined hands together to celebrate the Fourth and greet our boys just returned from the Army. The day opened with one hundred guns fired by the Battery boys, the many bells of the village rang forth a merry peal, and not unlike the old bell of '76, sounded forth the glad tidings, "Liberty throughout the Land, to all the inhabitants thereof." The Old Flag hung high, and looked gay as it was unfurled to the breeze from the many liberty poles, churches, dwellings and other places. The music of the Bands as they played the national airs, and the beating of the drums inspired

97

everyone and made all feel the great day had come, the day of jubilee, the time for rejoicing, the anniversary of our Nation's birthday, greeted with more joy then ever, that the War was over, the boys home and America free. At ten o'clock the procession formed, and marched through the principal streets of the village to the grove*. The most interesting feature of it was the appearance of our returned soldiers, who had borne the heat of battle and marched over many hundreds of miles of Southern soil. First came the infantry, then the battery boys with four pieces of artillery, their fine appearance, soldier-like bearing commanded the attention and remark of everyone. The Temperance Benevolent Society, connected with the Catholic Church, also presented a fine appearance in the procession with their banners flying, and beautiful red, white and blue badges—they turned out in large numbers and are deserving of much credit. All passed along well until they arrived at the grove, where a large fort was erected. Presently an armed force, said to be rebels, made their appearance in the fort with two pieces of artillery, and with a loud cheer unfurled a regular "secesh" flag, and planted it defiantly on the parapet of the fort. The battery was commanded by Lieut. Farrand, dressed in full rebel uniform. At this point the excitement was great. Terror and dismay reigned for a time. Men, women and children fled in wild confusion to the north side of the canal. Shortly after, the Union forces hove in sight, threw out their line of skirmishers, formed a line of battle, and brought their artillery to play on the fort, and a general engagement took place amid the rattle of musketry, and the roar of cannon from both sides. The Union forces were twice repulsed, but rallied, made another attack, and with a yell and cheers charged the fort, and carried the works, taking prisoners of all who were inside. The rebel flag was torn down, and Sergt. Gordon, color bearer on many a battle field, planted the old stars and stripes on the parapet, and the Old Flag was run

*The "grove" mentioned several times in this story, was the area within the boundaries of the Morris Canal, Washington Street, Monroe Street, and back to a point near the yards and buildings of the Ironworks. It must be remembered that none of the embankment and railroad trestles existed until 1873, and the entire area with its trees and grass-covered expanse was used for all celebrations, picnics, etc.

up the liberty pole, nearby, amid the cheers of the soldiers and the people, and the playing of Yankee Doodle by the band. While the battle was raging, could be heard above it all the rebel commander giving orders in true Southern style, "Ha, men, look after those Yankees down thar on the left!" After laying down their arms, the "Johnnies" were marched out of the fort under the Old Flag, and paroled for good behavior in the future. We saw on the field Major Davis, of the 15th Regiment; Lieut. Gaines, 7th Regt.; Captain Hutt, Lieuts. Miers, Milner and Sowley, of the First Regt.; Captain Steventon and Lieut. Farrand of the Battery, all of whom have been through the smoke of many battlefields, and know what it is to smell gunpowder. We also observed on the field Capts. Plant and Carlough, and Lieuts. Drinkwater and Trumbor, who had many narrow escapes. The ground was well selected and gave our citizens a good and correct idea of a real battle. Soon after the fight, dress parade came off near the grove.

The exercises in the grove were full of interest—some five or six thousand people were gathered. A large platform had been erected and trimmed with evergreens, covered and festooned with National flags; the American Shield hung down from the curtain, and underneath was a beautiful portrait of Washington; on the right, one of the late President Lincoln, and on the left, one of General Grant; and below it all, in large letters, were the words, "Welcome! Defenders of our Flag!" The Band, under the leadership of Joseph Fitzpatrick, Esq., performed some choice music, and the Glee Club sang a beautiful patriotic piece suited for the occasion.

The oration, by Major Z. Pangbom, of New York City, was received with the greatest satisfaction, and frequently applauded as he poured forth his strains of patriotic sentiments. We were a highly favored people in having such an eloquent speaker.

In the afternoon, a dinner was provided for our returned soldiers, after which exercises were held at the stand, and Rev. C. H. Mandeville, of Newburgh, N.Y., and Rev. Mr. Jansen of Pompton, made addresses.

At sundown a National salute was fired with shotted guns, the battery boys firing at a target. The day closed with a fine display of fireworks, large bon-fires on the hilltops, and illumination. Not the slightest accident occurred—no drunkenness; it was a day of real enjoyment to all, and our "Boys in Blue" seemed to be delighted to be home once more on the Fourth of July. Their good behavior and appearance called upon them words of praise from many lips. May they live to enjoy and join many celebrations of the Fourth of July, and their days of peace and happiness be as many and great as their deeds have been grand and glorious.

The net proceeds of the celebration amounted to the net sum of Thirteen Hundred Dollars, to be appropriated towards erecting a monument in this Town to the memory of our departed heroes who have fallen in defense of our Country and Its Flag.[184]

The Soldier's Monument

The Fourth of July celebration of 1865 was an excellent illustration of the spirit that prevailed in "Old Pequannoc." This display of gratitude by our citizens, and the show of affection of the returned soldiers for their people was demonstrated to its fullest degree. The monument to our soldier dead and the events leading up to its dedication in 1876 are of more than passing interest.

The monument, when first proposed, caused considerable controversy, for there were persons not residents of Pequannock, who felt that we should divert our efforts toward a large County monument, to be erected on the "Green" in Morristown. But the citizens and veterans of Pequannock were firm in their decision and proceeded accordingly.

The thirteen hundred dollars that was raised at the Fourth of July Celebration in 1865 was invested at once in township and government bonds at six per cent, and the interest with additional sums kept invested until 1876, when it was found enough had accumulated for the purpose.

During this period Pequannock Township had been divided into smaller townships, Boonton, Montville and Pequannock, and the village of Boonton had become the Town of Boonton, having received its charter March 18, 1867.[185]

The Soldier's Monument.

Late in the year of 1875 a committee was selected by the citizens of these townships to find a site and erect a suitable monument. The following citizens were appointed: George W. Esten, Edwin E. Willis, J. H. Homan, Abram VanDuyne, Aaron VanDuyne, E. V. G. Van Saun, and Peter Hopper. The site for the monument was donated by the Fuller and Lord Estate; the contract to erect it was awarded to H. H. Davis, of Morristown.

The monument was described as being of Quincy granite, thirty-two feet high with an eight foot base, and the several inscriptions noted. Plans were made to have the monument completed and ready for dedication on July 4, 1876, in time for the observance of the Centennial year, and it was therefore to be known as the Centennial Monument. This name did not seem to suit our citizens for in all the references that followed, the monument was always referred to as the Soldier's Monument.[186]

The awaited day came, and once more our people demonstrated with such patriotic fervor the qualities that gave "Old Pequannoc" its place in history. Boonton by this time had a newspaper of its own, and the detailed account of the celebration, as recorded by Samuel L. Garrison, the editor and owner of the *Boonton Weekly Bulletin*, affords us with a very graphic description of the happenings of that day. Herewith is the article as it appeared in the July 6, 1876, issue of Mr. Garrison's paper:

FOURTH OF JULY, 1876
Boonton Celebrates the 100th Anniversary of Our
National Independence.

A Great Day.
The Soldier's Monument Dedicated.

Tuesday was a great day for this Nation. One hundred years previous the immortal Declaration of Independence was signed, and as the United States of America has existed for that length of time, everywhere the people commemorated the great and glorious event. Boonton was not behind the other towns and cities in celebrating the day. At 12 o'clock on Monday night, the boom of cannon awakened our citizens, and there was but little if any sleep after that hour. The day was ushered in with the firing of cannon, and at a very early hour not only the residents of the Town, but people from Montville, Hanover, Pequannock, Rockaway, Randolph and Morristown poured into this place. The Stars and Stripes waved proudly over many of our homes and business places. Along Main Street the tri-colors hung pendent from the stores or waved in the shape of little flags extended from the roofs. It was a beautiful sight and one that will long be remembered. As nearly all the towns in the Country presented a similar appearance, it is hardly worth while to give an extended description for the benefit of the outside readers.

Shortly after eight o'clock the people commenced to assemble at the Soldier's Monument, which had been beautifully veiled with an American Flag. Opposite, the platform had been erected, and the names of "Pequannock," "Montville," and "Boonton," surrounded by evergreens, stood out boldly. About 10 o'clock the grand procession, headed by the Boonton Brass Band, started up Cornelia Street.

The Pequannoc Cavalry Company, led by William Milner and headed by the Color Bearer followed the Band Wagon.

The Marshal, Henry D. Crane, and his aides, S. S. Lyons, G. W. Jenkins, Rob't Green, E. B. Dawson and F. Jenkins were next in line.

Then came a magnificent representation of Columbus and his sailors. The characters were well represented —the costumes beautiful, and the whole scene attracting unusual attention.

The Pilgrim Fathers followed, adding to the interest of the presentation.

Then came a representation of William Penn and the Indian, signing the treaty, with other Indians, in the midst of whom was little Jersey Blue. The gentlemen representing the characters, as they went through the details of the treaty,

103

smoking the pipe of peace, etc., gazed at so pleasantly by the little girl representing New Jersey, were greeted with the huzzas of the mass of people lining the sidewalks.

Molly Pitcher, on horseback, holding the historical pitcher, which carried water to the brave artillerymen of Revolutionary and New Jersey fame, was an attractive feature. We did not hear anybody say, but took it for granted that the pitcher was the veritable one carried by the original Molly.

George Washington, accompanied by the Goddesses of Liberty, Truth and Justice, with War in the background, added to the grandeur of the parade.

Following came thirteen beautiful young ladies, handsomely attired in white, carrying shields, and in the same wagon was the bearer of a painting of the Bell of Independence, the historical crack was plainly visible. Then came twenty-five young ladies as handsome as the thirteen original colonies, bearing shields with the names of the other twenty-five States thereon. A beautiful banner, borne by four old residents of this section, gave the people to understand that the bearers were proud of their native township,—"Old Pequannoc."

The wagon containing "Young America" was not the smallest feature of the parade, notwithstanding the limited size of the occupants. The thirteen little boys with their flags, and a banner with the dates "1776-1876" singing "Hold the Fort," seemed to say that this young Republic was destined to exist still another century.

The Catholic School was represented by a respectable delegation of children.

After passing through the principal streets of the Town, the processions passed before the Monument and halted.

The programme of the Dedication was then gone through with. First came music by the Boonton Brass Band, followed with prayer by the Rev. D. E. Megie, and vocal music under the leadership of Mr. M. S. Shaw.

The Monument was then presented to the citizens of Old Pequannoc by Mr. George W. Esten, Chairman of the Committee. He gave a short history of the enterprise, stating that in 1865 a general celebration was held in Boonton, participated in by the citizens of three Townships. A sham battle was fought, in which the Union Troops not only captured the rebel battery, but seventeen hundred dollars as well. Since that time, the money having been well invested, had more than doubled. The Monument was erected by a grateful people in memory of those who fell on the field of battle, and was no less honorable because it was so long erected after the appropriation. It now cost 25 per cent less than it would have cost three years ago. The Monument cost $3,200, the foundation, fence and retaining wall nearly $600 more. He then in the name of the joint Committee, consisting of George W. Esten, E. E. Willis, J. H. Homan, Abraham C. VanDuyne, Aaron VanDuyne, Peter Hopper, and E. V. G. Van Saun, handed the Monument over to the people.

It was accepted by Judge John L. Kanouse, who was selected in behalf of the citizens of the three Townships, to receive it. Mr. Kanouse made an address exceedingly commendable in character. He noticed the growth of the Nation, the result of mental activity; the benefits of our free Government, the vastness of our Country, its prosperity, etc., were all alluded to, and then the mighty effort to destroy them by some of our countrymen rising in rebellion, the sacrifices and death of the men in whose memory the Monument had been erected. He then formally thanked the Committee for their labors.

At the close of the dedicatory exercises, the Monument was unveiled, and the procession started for the parade grounds.

The March down Main Street was very imposing. The music, the waving flags, the flaunting bunting, etc., made a scene very attractive. Near the Canal Bridge a beautiful banner was suspended, on which the motto: "A Republic One Hundred Years because of Loyal Sons." Over the motto was an eagle in gilt and surrounding it were stars representing the different States.

At the Celebration Grounds, a scene of activity was presented scarcely ever before witnessed in Boonton, and the stands, which were numerous, were doing a good business. Ice cream, Lemonade, Root Beer, Pineapples, Oranges, Bananas, Confectionery, Pies, Cakes, etc., were disposed of at a rapid rate.

Hundreds of people gathered at the speaker's stand. It was near noon when the exercises commenced.

After music by the Band an appropriate prayer was offered by the Rev. J. B. Taylor, followed by music.

Rev. J. H. Gunning, of Morristown was introduced and made a few remarks before reading the Declaration of Independence. His account of the scene at Independence Hall, when the blue-eyed boy told the old man in the belfry to ring, and the effort the old man made, was certainly inspiring. Mr. Gunning read the Declaration of Independence in an admirable manner. It was creditable to read it on our Centennial Anniversary.

The oration of Rev. A. J. Palmer, of New York City, entitled "The Growth of Man During the Last Century—Intellectually, Socially and Heroically" was one of the ablest we ever listened to. The orator was greeted with frequent applause as he portrayed evidence of advancement and told in language chaste and beautiful, the deeds of some of the noblest of American citizens, dead and living. It was oppressively warm, and as the speaker arose to the sublime point in his oration, in describing the heroic principles of man's growth in this Nation, illustrated in the recent war, he was overcome with the heat. Sitting down he said, "Let the Band Play, and I will finish." The Band played but the speaker was unable to proceed further. He recovered sufficiently to partake of some dinner, after which he looked much better and when he left on the 2:30 express for New York, was to all appearances as well as he came.

The exercises throughout were exceedingly interesting in their character. The exercises of the day closed with a display of fireworks in the evening.[187]

The Monument, once standing alone and impressive on the hillside, is now almost obscured by buildings nearby; people pass, unaware of its presence and significance. There are those who remember Memorial Days in the past, when a thin line of veterans, diminishing with the passing years, would stop and pay their respects to the memory of their departed comrades. They felt its presence, and they knew its significance.

Chapter V
Two Outstanding Leaders

The Hon. John Hill

The Hon. John Hill's participation in the affairs of "Old Pequannoc" and Boonton has been a considerable part of this story, and it demanded the recognition given. His exemplary

Hon. John Hill.

life and character that left its mark in the hearts of our people were also evident in his service in State and national affairs.

John Hill was not a native of this locality, being born in Catskill, New York, June 10, 1821.[188] He received a private school education, and at an early age worked in the bank where his father was cashier. Here he was taught bookkeeping. He came to Boonton in 1845, and accepted the position of paymaster at the Ironworks. Shortly after, he entered in the business of a general store, working with different partners for short durations until his association with William C. Lathrop. This store, located on Plane Street adjoining the Ironworks office, was called the John Hill & Co. "Empire Store," and served the mill workers and the Town until the Ironworks ceased operations in 1876. There was also a branch store on the corner of Liberty and Birch Streets.

John Hill was appointed postmaster of Boonton in 1849, and served until 1854. In 1852 he was elected to the Township Committee and was reelected every year until 1856. He was again elected to that post in 1863, continuing until 1867, serving a total of eight years. During this time he also served as Justice of the Peace for five years.

In 1861 and 1862 he was chosen a member of the House of Assembly, but was defeated for the State Senate in the fall of '62. It was said he neglected his campaign, preferring to give his attention to the war activities of the Township. While in Trenton he was a member of the Committee on Reception to Abraham Lincoln, when Lincoln stopped at Trenton on his way to Washington for his inauguration to the Presidency.

With the war at an end, he again turned to political life, and in the fall of 1865 he was nominated and elected to the House of Assembly for his third term. His activities during the war were well known and his popularity made the contest a mere formality.

The delegates to the Union Convention of Morris County assembled in Washington Hall at Boonton, October 28, 1865, and endorsed John Hill's candidacy by a unanimous vote. No other name was mentioned.[189] The delegates of the Essex

County Convention, also of the Second Assembly District, concurred with the action taken by the Morris County delegation in their selection of John Hill, and in a communication there were expressions of "We send you our most hearty greeting, we give you our most hearty thanks . . ." and "We bid All Hail to Old Pequannoc." The Essex group made references to John Hill's ability as a debater, and his record as a "leading member" of the House of Assembly, and also predicted his being selected as the next Speaker of the House.'[90]

When the House of Assembly entered in session, January, 1866, John Hill was elected Speaker and his acceptance speech was carried in all the newspapers.

John Hill's term as Speaker of the House of Assembly was brought to a close when he decided to enter into national politics. That his service as Speaker met with the approval of a large majority of the citizens of the District was confirmed in an article in *The Jerseyman*:

SPEAKER HILL

It is the universal testimony of those familiar with our State Legislatures, that the Speakership of the House of Assembly was never filled as capably and acceptably than during the last session by Hon. John Hill, of this County. We feel extremely gratified that such is the fact. It is honorable to him, and creditable to the County whose representative he is. Knowing Mr. Hill's ability and integrity, his qualifications of head and heart, we urged him warmly for that position, in the full confidence that he need only to be better known to be more highly appreciated, and that he would prove himself equal to all the requirements of that post of responsibilities and duty. An honest man, an enterprising citizen, a sympathetic, true hearted friend, a Christian gentleman in the full sense of the term, we feel sure there are other fields of honor and usefulness yet before him.

The following proceedings of the House in reference to him, with some introductory remarks from the State Gazette, will be read with pleasure by his friends at home:

We give below the resolutions passed by the House of Assembly, in honor of the upright and honorable course of John Hill, the Speaker during the legislative session just closed. Mr. Hill received the commendations of the members of both political parties, for the impartial and able manner in which he has presided over the deliberations of this session of the Assembly. It is a noteworthy fact, that without collusion, some half dozen members had resolutions strongly endorsing the Speaker, ready to offer at the same time. Gen. Ramsey's came first, then Mr. Lathrop's, and others. We mention this as an indication of the high appreciation entertained for Mr. Hill by all. Mr. Hill has also, won golden opinions for himself among the people of this city. We regret his departure from among us. We give below the resolutions adopted by the Assembly.

WHEREAS, We are about to adjourn after a lengthy and excited session, and it is but just and proper that this House should express its appreciation of the distinguished and eminent abilities of the Speaker in performing the manifold and arduous duties of his position,

Therefore Resolved, That the thanks of this House be and are hereby tendered to the Hon. John Hill, Speaker of the House, for the faithful and impartial manner in which he has presided over the deliberations of this body, during the present session, and further,

Resolved, That after the social separation that is about to take place, as members of this House of Assembly, we will still cherish with profound respect the kindness and affability of the Speaker in his social relations with the members.[191]

John Hill's acknowledgment of the foregoing resolutions was executed in oratory impeccable, yet unassuming. He concluded his reply with,

. . . For my part, gentlemen, I shall ever cherish with satisfaction the recollection of this session, and the friendship which it has knit about my heart. In whatever path of life it may be my lot hereafter to walk, I shall always follow with interest the career of each and every member of this House.

The hours of labor here, gentlemen of the Assembly, are numbered. I thank you again for your constant kindness and courtesy, and invoke upon all the blessings of that Cod whose love and care are ever about us, smoothing the paths before our feet.[192]

On September 5, 1866, at a convention of delegates representing the Fourth Congressional District, held at Liberty Hall, Orange, N.J., John Hill was unanimously nominated the Republican Union candidate to represent this District in Congress.[193]

The period marking the campaign of John Hill was highlighted by several noticeable aspects. There were those who opposed his election to the State Assembly who were now strongly supporting him for Congressman. There wasn't any question regarding the soldiers' vote for all over the District "Union" men formed organizations and supported Mr. Hill in every way possible.

In Boonton, the "Soldier's National Union," under the leadership of Charles A. Norris, met in Washington Hall and adopted resolutions pledging support to Mr. Hill. The soldiers of Morristown and vicinity—"who are in favor of the election of that tried and true friend of the soldiers, John Hill," were requested to meet and form a Campaign club. A long list of their names was included in a published report.[194]

Many miles were traveled with horse and wagon to bring Mr. Hill to the voters, and as one source relates, "His stirring speeches in every village and crossroads awakened enthusiasms never witnessed in previous political campaigns." [194]

John Hill was victorious by a majority of 465 votes over his opponent, Andrew J. Rogers, carrying eight of the twelve townships and three of the five counties in the District. The majority in Pequannock was 565.[195]

This was the first of three successive terms in Congress for John Hill, spanning the years of 1867-1873. During the three terms he was a member of the Committee of Post Offices and Post Roads, and it was largely due to his efforts that the postal-card system was adopted and franking privileges abolished.[197]

In the fall of 1874, despite a "Democratic tidal wave, he was elected to the State Senate, receiving in Boonton the unprecedented majority of four hundred and six. In 1880 he was again elected to Congress, defeating Augustus W. Cutler, of Morristown, by sixteen hundred votes. It was during this term that Mr. Hill was successful with his bill to reduce letter postage from three to two cents. He was opposed in this measure by Congressman James A. Garfield, who later became President. It was said of Mr. Hill's efforts, "He displayed an earnestness and perseverance in the matter that called forth universal commendation. No obstacles prevented Mr. Hill pressing to a successful termination of any act which he considered of public importance." [198]

It had been John Hill's ambition and desire to become Governor of the State, and few men ever had stronger support than he, but owing to his declining health, he was dissuaded by his doctors from entering the rigors of another campaign or office.[199]

With all the demands that his public activities imposed upon John Hill he did not permit them to relegate his religious life into secondary importance. He had been a member of the Presbyterian Church at Catskill, New York, and on coming to Boonton, his letter was received by the Presbyterian Church here. The first Sunday found him in the Sabbath school, and only a short time elapsed before he was given a class. His ability to teach proved a valuable asset to the school and shortly after he was chosen Superintendent, serving in that capacity for about thirty-five years. Many of Boonton's citizens were thankful for Mr. Hill's early guidance and instruction, for it had a marked effect on their thoughts and way of life. Soon after his arrival here he became an Elder of the Church, and continued as such for thirty-nine years. His Christian activities were many. He was prominent in the Young Men's Christian Association, attending conferences and conventions throughout the State and Country. He also served as a delegate to the Raike's Centennial, in London, to

John Hill Residence.

observe the celebration of the institution of Sunday Schools, and his account was published and read with great interest.[200] One of his last services was the delivery of an impressive address before the Presbyterian General Assembly, at Saratoga, N.Y., at which time he experienced his first symptoms of illness.[201] The last religious act of his life was addressing an anniversary gathering of the Sunday School, where every heart was touched and every eye was moistened as he spoke to the School for the last time.[202]

During the weeks following this occurrence he would sit on the spacious porch of his residence, on the corner of Birch and Cornelia Streets. There he would talk to his many friends who were concerned about him; at times he would ride out in his carriage to see the places and friends that were his very existence. He was confined to his bed but a short time when he passed away, July 24, 1884.

On the day of John Hill's burial, an Honor Guard of the John Hill Post, G.A.R., standing shoulder to shoulder, reached from the door of his home to the sidewalk and up to the entrance of the Presbyterian Church, to pay their last respects to their friend, as the pallbearers carried his remains to the Church for the service.[203]

John Hill Memorial monument.

In the Boonton Cemetery on the hill, there stands a monument, straight and tall; it tells of one who was loved and revered by his fellowmen. Around it are the many graves of soldiers and friends he knew and labored with, all being a part of the drama just reviewed. This monument, dedicated Decoration Day, May 30, 1885, was a joint memorial from ninety-four Sunday Schools of all denominations in this County.[204] It marks the grave of John Hill, citizen, patriot, disciple.

John L. Kanouse

Among those men who gained recognition and drew the attention of the people during this era in Boonton's history there was still another man with the Christian name of John.

John L. Kanouse.

115

There was Dr. John Grimes, whose labors in the Anti-Slavery movement brought acclaim to him and his associates. There was John Hill, whose patriotism was exceeded only by his beneficence. And there was John L. Kanouse.

It was John L. Kanouse's contribution to our system of public schools, and his writings of local history that brought to him the gratitude and respect of all those who enjoy the product of his labors, preserving for posterity the history of Boonton and neighboring places.

It is unusual, and almost without exception, that all the historical references to John L. Kanouse were written by himself, but in so doing Mr. Kanouse brought attention to himself with reluctance and hesitation, for his writings proved him to be an extremely modest person and he used his name only when it was necessary to do so.

John L. Kanouse came from emigrant stock. His grandfather, Jacob Kanouse, came to America with his brother Heinrich, from Wurtenburg, Germany, about 1750. Jacob settled near Boonton prior to 1766; his house is still standing and occupied by his descendants at Powerville. A son, Abraham, married Elizabeth Low, and John L. Kanouse was born of this marriage, February 17, 1811, at the farmstead of his maternal grandfather, John Low. It is believed that the stone house on the corner of Lathrop Avenue and Wilson Street, known as the Banta House, is the birthplace of Mr. Kanouse. In 1819, his mother, sister and brother died of a prevailing epidemic, leaving the father and son to mourn their loss.

Mr. Kanouse acquired his early education in the public schools near here (possibly Montville), and at age thirteen he entered the private school at Succasunna, under the tutelage of Ezra Fairchild. At seventeen he became a student in the Bloomfield Academy, attending the school for one year. He then turned his attention to teaching, but later, in 1830, he resumed his studies, entering Union College, Schenectady, N.Y., as a member of the junior class. In July 1832 he was graduated with the degree of Bachelor of Arts, and the following year was honored with the degree of Master of Arts.[205]

Birthplace of John L. Kanouse, Lathrop Ave., Boonton.

A few years after leaving college he entered in business, and his extensive properties in the easterly part of the town were always referred to as the Kanouse Farm. The older citizens can remember Mr. Kanouse's home located about midway between the present Kanouse and Roessler Streets, and about fifty yards in from the Newark Turnpike, later named Lathrop Avenue. It was quite large, built of red brick, with large chimneys and a Dutch gambrel roof. It had a solitary, imposing appearance, for standing amid cultivated fields it enjoyed the entire landscape by itself. The farm was not his primary activity, for he operated a general food and supply business located on Main Street, opposite Myrtle Avenue. The location was included in 1962 in the westerly approach to Highway 287. He also operated a coal yard on the bank of the Morris Canal about opposite the railroad station.[206]

He always had been a student of political questions, of social problems, and demonstrated a keen and sincere interest in the general needs of the Country and its people. His thorough understanding of these things had peculiarly fitted him for public office. His pronounced ability and profound interest did not go unnoticed by the people, for he was called to serve in many posts of public office.

He was elected to the office of superintendent of the public schools of Pequannock Township in 1847, and filled that office for twenty years. He was chosen in 1849 and again in 1852 to represent our district in the State Legislature. He was appointed to the committee on education in 1850, and prepared the School Bill that was presented and passed in 1851, which seems to have brought him his greatest notice. He became interested in prison reform while in the Legislature, and when he returned home, he prepared a report on the condition of the Morris County prison. The report was accepted and action was taken at once to improve our county institution. He served as Director of the Board of Freeholders for three years and, in 1872, was elected associate judge of Morris County and served in that capacity for five years. He served in various township offices, especially that of tax collector, holding that office until a few years before his passing. Mr. Kanouse made a practice of preparing charts and presenting them for comparative analysis to prove a point in question, and to demonstrate the course which should be followed to get the most from the tax dollar for the community [207]

John L. Kanouse recognized and met his obligations to public office in a conscientious and commendable manner, and served to the utmost of his capabilities. But it seems that education was his first love, and it was definitely in this subject that his forethought and influence evinced their greatest impact. The Boonton School became the striking example of his planning and conception.

It was in the latter part of January, 1876, that Judge Kanouse, as he was called by all who knew him, was called upon by the Superintendent of Morris County Schools to write a history of the public schools in the three townships of Pequannock, Montville and Boonton. It was to be used for an exhibit in the educational department of the Centennial Exhibition to open in May at Philadelphia. Although the time to prepare it was brief, Mr. Kanouse completed the history in ample time. The county superintendent, L. W. Thurber, had it engrossed and it appeared in its proper place at the Centennial.

A few years ago the original engrossed manuscript of this excellent reference was found in the Special Collections in the Rutgers University Library, and a reproduction was made for the writer by Dr. Donald A. Sinclair, Curator of Special Collections, at Rutgers. Mr. Kanouse's contribution extended over fifty large pages, or better than half of the entire composition, and from it portions will be extracted for our present purpose.[208]

Mr. Kanouse tells us that "The oldest record of Pequannock Township that we find in the keeping of the township clerk bears the date 1741, which was in the fourteenth year of the reign of George II, King of England. This was no doubt the first record of the township proceedings after the separation of Pequannock from Hanover Township which appears to have been done by the 'Court of General Sessions of the Peace,' March 25, 1740. The first record of the township book pertains to the election of township officers and the raising of money for the support of the poor, who in those days were farmed out to the lowest bidder. We find no record on the township books pertaining to educational matters as far back as this period or for 89 years thereafter, until 1830, when the first school system established by an act of the Legislature in 1829 went into effect."

Although present Boonton did not exist prior to 1829, the area was part of Pequannock Township, with several farmhouses on the easterly fringe of the area and a house or two at the foot of Sheep Hill. John L. Kanouse was 18 years old at this time and doing his best to acquire an education. He writes of this period and the year 1829, for it had a two-fold significance. It is the birth date of our town and it also marks a point that had state-wide educational importance.

Action was taken by our Legislature at the session in February, 1829, by which was established the first system of public instruction in the State of New Jersey. Briefly, under this act the people of the townships were authorized to raise money

119

by tax for the support of the schools; to appoint a committee of three charged with the duty of supervising the schools, and the examining and licensing of teachers. The school committees were chosen on a yearly basis. William Jackson of Rockaway, Samuel Bogert of Pompton Plains and Silas Cook of Montville, were the first school committee chosen.

The amount of public funds distributed under this system was small, only $20,000 for the whole State, which gave Moms County $1,568 for its share, and about sixty cents a child in Pequannock.[209]

In 1847 a new school law went into effect, giving the people power, though under restrictions, to raise larger amounts by township tax for the support of the schools. It also provided for the appointment of a township superintendent, in place of a committee of three. That school system, subject to some amendments, continued in force for twenty-eight years, until it was repealed by an Act of April 5, 1875. Under the Act of 1847, John L. Kanouse was chosen the first superintendent, and held that position from 1847 to 1867.[210]

Mr. Kanouse had many constructive ideas to bring before the people, but it took a great deal more than merely suggesting to the citizens the changes he deemed important. The old mode of employing teachers was still continued in many districts, and it interfered with securing and retaining the services of competent instructors. As a natural consequence there were frequent interruptions in keeping schools open, which encouraged partial attendance, all resulting in lack of interest. The dilapidated condition of many of the buildings, the lack of necessary facilities, the uncared-for condition of the surrounding playgrounds, and the uncomfortable school furnishings, all contributed to render the schools uninviting and decidedly unpleasant. To fulfill his intentions Mr. Kanouse was confronted with the enormous task of convincing the people and getting them to agree to his ideas for improvement.

The old-fashioned method of town meetings was still in use in Pequannock, with the people expressing themselves and voting from the floor. As such a meeting afforded a good opportunity to reach the attention of large numbers of people at one time, Mr. Kanouse prepared and read at such a meeting, in April 1850, a report setting forth the hindrances and improvements as he saw them, and urging the necessity of action on the part of the people, telling them the remedy was wholly with them. That report was favorably received, and several hundred copies were ordered printed. Subsequently within two years three new schools were erected, others were repaired, furnishings were replaced and many minor improvements were effected.[211]

In the year 1850, as a result of the growing population of Boonton, our school became overcrowded and some of the people were asking for a division of the district. Mr. Kanouse, aware of what had been done at Plainfield, Bloomfield, Salem and Bridgeton under special power given by the Legislature to establish free schools, and thinking it would be to the advantage of the people of Boonton to remain in one district, felt that the time was at hand to erect a new school to accommodate the increasing enrollment, and also have it a free school, to be supported by a self-imposed tax. Mr. Kanouse prepared the draft of a bill which he thought suitable to meet the wants of the case. In November 1850, he presented it for consideration at a public meeting called for the purpose, and accompanied it with a statement fully portraying the advantages of a free school. In his writings of this Mr. Kanouse said, "The proposition and the bill were favorably received." Knowing Mr. Kanouse's character, we would not expect him to say otherwise; but was it really that simple? Surely he must have had to present his case with all the fervor and eloquence he could muster. This was a big decision for a small village to make, especially when it was dependent on a single industry for a continuing revenue necessary to see it through. His proposal must have met with some opposition. However, we must accept Mr. Kanouse's unassuming account of the proceedings. The proposition and the bill as presented were favorably received, and after further consideration at subsequent meetings, and some amendments suggested and adopted, the bill, accompanied with a petition, was presented to the next Legislature. The bill was passed into law March 13, 1851, and went into effect immediately.

Under the new system, in April 1851, William G. Lathrop, James Holman and George W. Esten were elected the first Board of Trustees, and Henry W. Crane was chosen Clerk. During that year the New Jersey Iron Company donated a plot of ground at the present School Street site where a brick building of suitable size and two stories in height was erected and completed the early part of the following year. School was opened in it on July 19, 1852, under Alonzo B. Corliss, principal, and Miss Corliss, assistant. This was the first, and for many years the only free school established in Morris County. It was kept free and regularly opened during the whole of each year, and, excepting its proportionate share of the State appropriation of public funds, was entirely sustained by money derived from taxes voluntarily imposed by the people of the district.[212]

That our new school, along with its new concepts on instruction and supervision, must have met with the approval of our people, there is no doubt, although Mr. Kanouse does not exert himself to draw attention to this. It did, however, receive notice from the editor of *The Jerseyman*. Morristown was having its troubles with the children who were not made to attend school regularly. Letters to the editor of *The Jerseyman* carried charges of neglect and improper teaching methods against those responsible for the educating of the children, and further charged this neglect encouraged "rowdyism," with the suggestion the "strong arm of the law should punish them." In commenting on the charges made, the editor agreed with the correspondent, and suggested that he continue to "keep it before the people," and "talking it up in the social circle." Editor Vance concluded the item with the following comment: "We rarely have occasion to feel ashamed of the enterprise of our town, but we must confess that a tinge of something of that description mantled our cheek a few days since, while looking at the exterior and interior of the Public School House in Boonton. We do not propose to describe it, but we respectfully suggest that any of our citizens who may chance to be at that place, pay it a visit. To say that Boonton contains little, if any, more than half the population of Morristown, and not a quarter of its wealth, while its facilities for common school instruction are immeasurably in advance of ours, will give an inkling of what every person will feel upon a survey of the two places with reference to this matter. Cannot something be done toward placing this Town in the front rank at least of the villages of Morris County in providing the means for the education of its children? Who will point out the best course to be pursued to secure it?" This article must have afforded our citizens moments of well deserved pride after reading it, and realizing their action had met with the approbation of the Morristown editor.[213]

In 1853, an association of the teachers of Pequannock Township was formed, with the object of self-improvement in matters pertaining to teaching as the primary function. Mr. Kanouse, serving as moderator, presided over their monthly meetings at the teachers' request.[214]

We can assume that the school served the calculated needs of the community through the 1850's, but later, with the prosperity of the Ironworks during the war years and the resultant rapid growth of Boonton, much of the population had spread beyond the limits of the school district as set forth by the Act of 1851. The school could not continue to accommodate the increasing enrollment, and the need for enlarging the facilities became imperative. Hence two additions, previously mentioned, were built in the 1860's.

The increased number of classes, or departments as they were then called, and the larger number of pupils, made it not only necessary to extend the boundaries of the district, but advisable to vest the management and control in a Board of Education, consisting of seven commissioners in place of the three trustees, and also to include provision for evening schools, for the accommodation of those whose occupations prevented their attendance at the day school.[215]

As already noted, John L. Kanouse became Superintendent of Schools in Pequannock Township in 1847, and we can be sure he gave special attention to the school he helped to plan and establish. However, with the separation from Pequannock Township, and the incorporation of the Town of Boonton in March 1867, Mr. Kanouse no longer served as superintendent. He did, however, serve on the Board of Trustees of schools in Boonton, in the years that followed. The citizens well remembered his service in drafting the Act of 1851, establishing the free school in Boonton that commanded such well deserved attention. Therefore twenty years later, John L. Kanouse was again called upon to draft a new bill, providing for the necessary changes and the prospective wants of this growing community. In December 1874 a bill with suitable provisions was prepared, and the bill and petitions were presented to the Legislature at its next session. The bill received favorable action and became law, going into effect April 5, 1875.[216]

To put the former Harrison Street School in its proper place in this review, we must go back to 1874. The area known as the "Flats" or South Boonton, as well as the adjoining part of the township, was being served by old School House No. 6. This small school house, situated on present Lathrop Avenue, a short distance from the corner of Lathrop and Vreeland Avenues, was in use since 1844, when District No. 6 was formed.[217]

In 1874, the school trustees proposed replacing the little school with a larger building, and at a meeting in April of that year, a resolution was voted on and passed that permitted raising the amount of $3,600 by taxes for the erection of a new building. There was some opposition to the plan, the location and size of the school lot being termed objectionable. In June, at a special meeting called for the purpose, the following resolution was offered to the voters:

124

Whereas the school lot now owned by District No. 7 is too small, and does not provide room for playground and other purposes.

Resolved, that the legal voters of said district hereby authorize the Board of Trustees to effect an equal exchange with Abram P. Jacobus, Rachel Mandeville, Martha E. Dixon, and Sarah J. Demarest, and all others interested, for a lot on the corner of Harrison and Madison Streets, 150 feet on Harrison and 125 feet on Madison, and the Board to have full control in the arrangement of papers as will guarantee the entire surrender of the parties above named of all their rights and title in the lot on the corner of said Streets, and will convey it to the District without any charge outside of the transfer of the lot now owned by School District No. 7, it being understood that the building now standing on the school lot shall not be exchanged with the lot.

The citizens voted favorably on the proposal, and the exchange of lots was executed. With the acquisition of the Harrison Street property, a school of larger proportions than originally planned was agreed upon, and work commenced on it in September. The Harrison Street School was completed and ready for use in January, 1875.

It may be of interest to learn that old School House No. 6 was disposed of at public sale in December, 1874. It was purchased by William Lathrop and later sold to a Mr. Purcell. The new owner moved it intact to a new location. It was raised up to allow a story to be built underneath the old school building. In later years an addition was made and with alterations it was converted into a four-family residence. It can be found about midway between the Boonton High School and the John Hill School, at 319 Lathrop Avenue. The arched lintel over the windows in the upper sides of the building will identify the portion of the structure that was old School House No. 6.

John L. Kanouse completes his history of the Boonton School in Munsell's *History of Morris County* by referring to the Act of 1875, and by describing our school as it was at the time of his writing, in 1881:

Under this special act the school at Boonton is now operated. This school is graded, and occupies two buildings, one, the main building, in the north part of the town, and the other, a primary department in the south part. There are in all nine departments, under the charge of a principal and nine assistants. Both buildings are of brick, with slate roofs and two stories in height, and supplied with improved furniture . . . . The school property in Boonton is estimated to be worth $25,000.[218]

Mr. Kanouse closed his comments with this observation:

The experience of thirty years under the operation of a free school at Boonton has convinced the people there that no town becomes the poorer by taxing itself to educate its children; that a proper and thorough system of education will raise its moral, social and intellectual position, and add to the security and value of property, and that by consolidation and keeping strength together, better school and increased means of instruction can be secured, not only at comparatively less cost, but with far greater advantages.[219]

In the years that followed, John L. Kanouse kept in close touch with the affairs of the school and the town in general. He continued in business and the operation of the farm, and although he did not again seek public office, he did hold the appointment of tax collector until his 90th year.

Notwithstanding the unfortunate circumstance of his breaking an arm in the fall of 1904, his interest never faltered, and at a birthday party, celebrating his 94th year in 1905, we find him receiving his friends and enjoying their company. Our local editor reported that "Mr. Kanouse spent his time in reading and writing, and that he had quite a correspondence," also stating that "he had piles of manuscript of his own composition lying on his desk."

What a remarkable period he was able to witness! In his boyhood he could hear firsthand the stories of men who had fought in the Revolution. He could remember the digging of the Morris Canal, and seeing the first boats on their way to Paterson, Newark and Jersey City, long before the advent of the railroad. He witnessed the construction of the Ironworks and saw it develop into an industry of national importance. He saw a town born and grow into maturity. He saw our school grow from a single room in a dwelling-house near the mill into an institution of standing and reputation.

John L. Kanouse left this life August 5, 1905. He was born February 17, 1811. From 1811 to 1905, Mr. Kanouse had lived through a most eventful period in our history, and as a result of his observation and careful thought, he contributed greatly to the general improvement of our way of life. He had lived a life of service and dedication, for he gave of himself and his substance to those he met along the way.

Chapter VI
Depression Comes to Boonton

The Aftermath of the War

In reviewing the story of the founding and the establishment of Boonton, the years leading up to the war, the problems and situations confronting the people, the war itself and the participation of our citizens, the celebrations, the recognition of our war heroes, and the dedication of the Soldier's Monument, all these facts of our history have been described in phrases glamorized with expressions such as pioneering, enterprising, patriotic, heroic, dedicated and even romantic. How else could that period be described?

The period after the Civil War was quite different. The community known as Boonton was situated in the two townships of Pequannock and Hanover. Although no record was found that indicated conflicting situations in the government of the two townships, this might have been the reason for the change.

On March 18, 1867, the Legislature of the State of New Jersey passed an Act declaring that "all those parts of the Townships of Pequannock and Hanover, in the County of Morris, situate, lying and being within" certain described boundaries, "shall be and the same are hereby constituted, ordained and declared to be a town corporate, and shall henceforth be called, known and distinguished by the name of 'the Town of Boonton.' " [220]

For a few brief years the prosperity of the town continued with slight variation until 1874. On August 24, 1873, a big fire destroyed a large portion of the Ironworks. The lower nail factory, with sawmill connected, three large store houses, three sheds and several smaller buildings were destroyed along with their contents, machinery, etc. The turbulence created by the fire itself was so great that large embers were carried over the south end of the town, setting numerous small fires including one on the roof of the Reformed Church.[221] These were extinguished by citizens in the area. The mill buildings were replaced the same year and operations were continued with varying degree until 1876.[222]

In 1874 a cut in wages was effected, and there were layoffs at the mills. This tended to deplete whatever savings the workers had. Also, there were homes and properties not entirely paid for, resulting in foreclosures by those who held the mortgages.[223]

When one recalls to mind the account of the Centennial Celebration on July 4th of the same year, it is hard to conceive that it took place with full knowledge of the outlook of having Boonton's main source of support closing down.[224] The Mill owners, Dudley B. Fuller and James Couper Lord, died in 1868 and 1869 respectively. In surviving his associate, Mr. Lord came into sole possession of the real estate, including the mills, furnaces, mines and other property. In provisions stipulated in their wills, the Works continued in operation until 1876.[225]

Boonton's First Silk Mill

A group of citizens concerned themselves with the problems of the persons affected by the layoffs and a decision was made to find a way to provide work for the idle. The result was the building and establishment of Boonton's first Silk Mill. It was located between Mechanic and Division Streets, east of Cedar Street. The following extracts from the *Boonton Weekly Bulletin* are descriptive of the planning and results of the enterprise:

NOTICE

The subscribers to the fund to erect a building in which to manufacture silk goods are hereby requested to meet at the office of Mr. John VanOrden, corner of Main and Mechanic

130

Sts., tomorrow evening (Friday) for the purpose of electing three Trustees to take charge of the funds, purchase a lot, erect a building, and have the necessary papers made out to hold the property for a term of five years.

September 16, 1875.   S. L. Garrison, Secretary[226]

THE DEDICATION OF THE SILK FACTORY

Large Crowd Present—Great Enthusiasm

On Saturday afternoon last, the new silk factory in this place was formally dedicated and the corner stone placed in position. The meeting was called to order at 3 o'clock, by Mr. J. A. VanOrden, President of the Board of Trustees. After making a few introductory remarks, he introduced Mr. S. L. Garrison, Secretary of the Board, who gave a short history of the rise and progress of the enterprise. The Secretary read the list of subscribers and the agreement as made with Mr. James Sansfield, who is to occupy the factory. Mr. Sansfield agrees, in consideration of the fact that the property is to be his at the expiration of five years, to employ an average of twenty-five employees for each working day and during each year of the first two years, and an average of thirty-five employees for every working day during each and every year of the three succeeding years. Mr. Sansfield intends to employ hands sufficient to run both rooms, about one hundred and fifty, but was not willing to agree to that by signing a paper, as he could not read the future. He will place forty looms in as soon as the heating apparatus is in position.

After music by the Washington Cornet Band, the Chairman introduced Hon. A. W. Cutler, Member of Congress from the Fifth District, who addressed the gathering.

Hon. John Hill was also introduced and spoke of American industry in general.

The Secretary then announced the articles placed in the tin box for the corner stone. They were as follows:

List of the subscribers to the Silk Fund, Copies of the Boonton Bulletin, copies of the N.J. Freeman (published in Boonton in 1846), *New York Tribune*, a small pictorial newspaper, a poster announcing the dedication, Republican and

131

Democratic tickets, a blank certificate of stock, U.S. coin (one cent) dated 1875, and an English coin, dated 1870.

At the close of the meeting in the factory, the corner stone was placed in position, the Band playing, thus ending the festivities.[227]

November 11. 1875.

The plans of the Committee were carried out and a building thirty feet by seventy feet and two stories high was erected. The building was let to a Mr. Sansfield who proposed to start silk weaving. It soon turned out Mr. Sansfield was not the man for the place, and the project failed, much to the disappointment and injury of those who started it. There the matter rested for several years until the mill was taken over by the firm of Pelgram & Meyer of Paterson.[228]

Under the management of Pelgram & Meyer in the spring of 1880, the mill began operation with a few hands. By the end of the year the mill was extended by an addition of one hundred feet of building and employed about one hundred and thirty hands.[229]

Silk Mill.

In June of 1881 ground was broken for Pelgram & Meyer's new Silk Mill on Monroe and Lincoln Streets. When completed the building was forty feet by two hundred feet and four stories high.[230] To expand the facilities Pelgram and Meyer leased the second and third floors of the Hodgkins building, known today as the Ball building, located on Main Street opposite the foot of Boonton Avenue. This space accommodated thirty additional looms. It was reported that about one hundred and fifty were employed at the silk factory and the new mill would accommodate five or six hundred hands.[231] The ensuing years brought reports of expansion and improvements along with complaints of low wages and strikes by the workers. [232]

Charles Pelgram died in December, 1887, aged 43 years, and Isaias Meyer died in August, 1888, aged 75 years. Both gentlemen were afflicted with a heart ailment, probably brought about by the continual use of the long stairs in the new factory.[233]

Through the years following the passing of Messrs. Pelgram and Meyer, their successors continued in operation under the name of Pelgram & Meyer until the closing of the Silk Mill in 1927-28. The Silk Mill did contribute to Boonton's economy, which was the intention and hope of those citizens who conceived the original plan and who gave generously to its inception.

Boonton's Darkest Hour

In the Fall of 1876, the Boonton Ironworks closed, and operations ceased. It is believed that Mrs. Lord, in whose hands rested the control and direction of the Works, ordered the closing, despite the efforts and pleadings of the people. Meetings were held in Washington Hall in an attempt to find an answer to the disastrous state of affairs.

On a Saturday evening, August 24, 1876, in obedience to a call issued by a number of the employees of the Boonton

Ironworks, a large gathering of working men assembled in Washington Hall. Every seat was occupied and there was hardly standing room. The meeting was called to order by John Walley; Thomas Mains was elected chairman and George Anthony, secretary.

On taking the chair, Mr. Mains explained the object of the meeting, which was to take action on a petition to be presented to Mrs. Lord, or the Executors of the estate of the deceased James Couper Lord. The secretary then read the petition as it had been prepared to be presented to Mrs. Lord:

To Mrs. Lord,

Respected Madam,

The undersigned, employees of the late Boonton Nail Co., beg leave to make known to you the sad state into which they have been cast by the stoppage of these Works.

Boonton was once a flourishing village; its residents happy and content; its population increased rapidly; its homes were being constantly built up; and all this because of the employment given by the late lamented members of its Nail Co.— We still revere the names of the members of this Company because of their high-toned principles, and strict justice—as theirs under Providence we are indebted for the comforts and happiness of the past.

But alas! a dark—gloomy cloud has passed over our once favored and beloved village, enveloping its people with sadness and despair, for in the closing of Boonton's far famed factory, they see nothing but desolation . . . hunger.

Let us assure you, Respected Madam, that many of our families have, during the past month, derived their sustenance from berries gathered by day and fish caught by night. This is a sad state of things in free and great America, yet it is nevertheless too true.

We are satisfied that you are not aware of the extent of our sufferings, and we cannot blame anyone for their existence, but we beg to appeal to you in the name of our wives, in the name of our children, in the name of humanity and in the NAME OF GOD, to use your great influence that they be alleviated.

You are the owner of Boonton—it is your village; Oh! protect it and its people by the resumption of the works of its great factory. One word from you will suffice to put all its machinery in motion again. Oh! speak the word, Respected Madam, and receive the benedictions, the blessings, the thanks, the gratitude and affections of your own people.

Boonton, August 26th, 1876

At the meeting of August 26th, after reading the petition, George Anthony, Thomas Mains and John Walley were appointed a committee to present the petition to Mrs. Lord.

This petition, beautifully engrossed, is now in the collections of the Boonton Historical Society. It is evident that Mrs. Lord did not give the petition consideration, and it must have been returned, unanswered.

The committee had tried to arrange an interview with Edward C. Lord, executor of the Lord Estate, and they were rebuffed for their effort. The following communications were given in a report in the *Bulletin*.

TO THE WORKINGMEN OF BOONTON

Your Committee, appointed at the meeting held Saturday evening, August 26th, do now report that they have endeavored to perform the duties as the meeting directed. The following correspondence will show the result of their labor:

To Edward C. Lord, Executor of the Estate of the late James Couper Lord:

Dear Sir: At a meeting of the workmen late in the employ of the Boonton Iron Company, held on Saturday evening, August 26th, the workingmen there assembled appointed a Committee, consisting of Thomas Mains, George Anthony and John Walley, to present to Mrs. Lord, the owner of the Boonton fronworks, a petition signed by them; and also, to have an interview with one or more of the Executors of the Estate of our late respected employer, James Couper Lord. The Committee have sent to Mrs. Lord, a letter to the same effect as this.

—Will you please give the Committee an interview? The day and the hour most convenient to you will be the same for the Committee.

We are, very truly, your ob't servants,

George Anthony
Thomas Mains

Boonton, N.J. August 28, 1876.

The following discouraging reply was received:

Morristown, N.J.
August 30th, 1876.

Messrs. Ceo. Anthony, Thos. Mains, John Walley, Committee:

Gentlemen:
I have received your letter of the 28th instant. The executors of the Estate of Mr. J. Couper Lord are, at present, somewhat scattered, and I am unable to appoint any time at which it would be convenient for them to meet you. Any communication you may have to make to us you can make through W. G. Lathrop, who is in charge of the property, and I will be happy to submit it to the other Executors when an opportunity may arise.

I desire to inform your Committee that Mrs. J. Couper Lord has nothing to do with the management of this property, and it is scarcely worth while to annoy her with matters of business over which she has no control.

Resp'y
E. C. Lord

George Anthony
Thos. Mains
John Walley, Committee.[234]

Boonton, Sept. 5, 1876.

By the end of the year the situation in Boonton had reached a low point, when a Committee was appointed to "take control of the relief of the destitute" and a circular was distributed throughout the County asking for help.

AN APPEAL

FOR THE

POOR OF BOONTON !

The undersigned, a Committee appointed to take control of the relief of the destitute in Boonton, N. J., would make the following appeal to the charitable :

The village of Boonton, now numbering some 3,500 people, has grown up around the Boonton Iron Works. These Works have always been the sole dependence of the place. After running on short time for nearly two years, they are now, and have been for six months, entirely closed. The distress which this condition of things causes, during this severe Winter, to very many workingmen and their families, may be readily imagined. All are seeking work. A few are able to find employment from day to day ; but the depression which exists everywhere, prevents the most of them from getting work in other places, and therefore the whole village finds its income stopped—its supplies cut off. As the Boonton Iron Works were its *sole* dependence, there are very few persons in Boonton who now have the means to render any large assistance to the destitute. We feel therefore obliged, in our necessity, to ask help from abroad to assist us in providing the barest necessaries of life to the many who are thrown upon our care. The case is an extreme one ; it is absolutely a matter of life and death. Starvation must come to many families unless they are speedily helped by the charitable. We make an earnest appeal, therefore, to our friends and to the friends of the poor, to come to our aid in this hour of trial. Any contributions, either in money, provisions, clothing or fuel, will be thankfully received, and every exertion will be made to distribute them to those who need them most.

Money should be sent to the Treasurer, Mr. D. C. Ely; supplies will be received at the Union Store, kept by Mr. Chas. B. Norris, or the Committee will send for them when requested.

WM. G. LATHROP, Cha'n,	GEORGE FULLER,
JOHN HILL,	GEORGE W. ESTEN,
S. S. LYON,	PHILIP WOOTTON,
CHARLES B. NORRIS,	JAMES HOLMES,
JOHN L. KANOUSE,	JOHN I. KOPP,
H. C. JENKINS,	DUDLEY B. FULLER,
JOHN McELROY,	ARCHIBALD D. GREEN,
	COMMITTEE.

REV. J. P. APPLETON, CORRESPONDING SECRETARY.

BOONTON. N. J.. December 28th, 1876.

"Appeal for the Poor of Boonton."

137

Then the *Bulletin* explained how help was to be given:

The Committee appointed to select visitors for each district have performed their work. The following are those selected.

VISITORS

1st Dist., that part of Boonton known as the "Flats": D. D. Tompkins, Jr., John Stone, Mrs. C. D. Woodruff, Mrs. John Stone.

2nd Dist., from Canal Bridge to Division St.: J. D. Mockridge, Amzi Burroughs, Mrs. J. W. Richards, Mrs. E. A. Backer.

3rd Dist., Division to William Sts.: Wm. Grubb, John Sutton, Mrs. T. D. Gladson, Mrs. John Sutton.

4th Dist., William to Cornelia Sts.: Thos. Hammonds, Mrs. Wm. Gardner, Joseph Fitzpatrick, Mrs. Thomas Hammonds.

5th Dist., Cornelia to Church Sts.: Jos. Hodgkins, C. W. Esten, Mrs. William Grubb, Mrs. John Hill.

6th Dist., Church to Brook Sts.: N. A. Myers, Samuel Hammonds, Mrs. N. A. Myers, Mrs. Samuel Hammonds.

7th Dist., Brook to Liberty Sts.: R. S. James, John Jaques, Mrs. C. O. Cooper, Mrs. Vincent.

8th Dist., Liberty to Green Sts.: John W. Lee, Geo. Smith, Mrs. James Flemming, Mrs. Harry Lyon.

9th Dist., Green Street to North boundary line: Daniel Jones, Wm. Milner, Mrs. Daniel Jones, Mrs. Wm. Milner.

10th Dist., Between Plane and Main Sts.: Joseph Davis, Mrs. Joseph Davis.

11th Dist., West Boonton: James King, James Norris, Mrs. James King, Mrs. James Norris.

We understand it is not designed to canvass the districts, but for the visitors when applied to for relief to look to the necessities of the case and if the needs are such as to warrant, to fill up the blank form (printed for that purpose) of such things as are necessary, which articles will be furnished by the general committee.

There is no necessity for any family in the place suffering for the necessaries of life. We have understood there are some who are so sensitive about the matters as to neglect to state their real condition. To our mind this is foolish to say the least.—If we were in need, we would not hesitate one moment to let our wants be known.—We would live on very plain food it is true rather than to appeal to charity, but before we would suffer we most assuredly would state our condition and ask for relief.

We suggest to the visiting committees the necessity of understanding fully the condition of all who apply for relief. See if extravagance stands out boldly, and whether those who apply are really deserving. There are many worthy poor, who deserve help, and if their wants are known, will receive it. The committees are made up of persons who no doubt understand their business and we have no fears but what the deserving will be noted and the deserving assisted.

Let it be understood then that all who are in needy circumstances are to make application to the visiting committee in the district where they reside.[235]

Having the opportunity of interviewing Miss Jessie Phillips on the occasion of her hundredth birthday, the question was asked if she had any recollection of the hard times after the Civil War. "My, yes!" she replied. "My father had bought a small farm down in Old Boonton, and as a little girl I can remember people from Boonton who came walking along the road and asking the farmers for food for their children. I remember this because it made me very sad, and I cried." Miss Phillips was 106 years old when she died, November 12, 1970.[236]

The Decline of the Boonton Ironworks

It must have been a time of bewilderment and consternation that confronted the workmen of Boonton. To ponder over the diminishing possibilities of the Ironworks ever returning to its former status must have been discouraging. Long lists of names of the men working on the streets of Boonton were published in the local paper. These men were given a credit on their tax bill, hoping they could save their homes in this manner.[237] In contrast to this these men could read of the activity occurring elsewhere in the County and State. Some of the more venturous workmen left Boonton to find jobs in these places.

Herewith are examples of the notices found in the *Bulletin*:

A number of Boonton families have recently moved to Bloomingdale. The rubber works there is in full operation.[238]

Oxford has fewer unemployed men now than in any other time during 1873. All the works are going full time.[239]

•　　　•　　　•

Boonton workmen are slowly finding employment elsewhere. A number more—we understand sixteen in all—have been employed by Cooper & Hewitt at Trenton. It will be a great day for this section when our first class mechanics and workingmen are permitted to go to work in our own establishment.[240]

•　　　•　　　•

New self-feeding machines in operation at Pottstown, Pa. They will cut 20% more nails than the older type machine.[241]

•　　　•　　　•

A letter from Pottstown, Pa., to Eli Worman at Boonton:

Sir: I was informed by a young man from Boonton that Feeders might be obtained there, and requested me to drop you a few lines in regard to it. We are going to run our works double turn and will need about twenty-five or thirty additional Feeders. We intend to start double turn next week, Monday, March 17th. Tell them to try and get here about that time, and oblige,

Pottstown Iron Works, per T. Searles.[242]

•　　　•　　　•

The Powerville rolling mill and forge are running full time. Mr. Leonard gives employment to quite a large number of men one way or another.[243]

In the Spring of 1879, along with the letter to Eli Worman, the following notice was found in the same issue of the Bulletin. It was the first of its kind since the closing of the Ironworks in 1876.

THE BOONTON IRON WORKS FOR SALE

The Boonton Iron Works have been put in the market and publicly offered for sale. It is said it will require $65,000 to put the works in order and start them. Their vastness may be imagined from the following schedule of the property:

Two Blast Furnaces, steam and water power, with all modern appliances. Capacity, 25,000 tons of metal per annum.

Puddling Mill, containing 12 double puddling and two scrap furnaces.

Plate Mill, containing five heating furnaces and two train of rolls.

Nail Factories, containing 150 machines.

Store House, with storage capacity for 50,000 kegs of nails.

Keg Factory, with machinery to produce 300,000 kegs per annum.

Machine Shop, Carpenter Shop, Plumber Shop, Foundry, etc.

All necessary machinery and appurtenances, driven by ample and unfailing water power, and exceptional advantages for coal, ore and transportation for production.[244]

The three year period of complete inactivity (1876-1879) had an adverse effect on the entire operation of the Boonton Ironworks. From the commencement these extensive ironworks constituted the one great industry and nearly the sole dependence of this place, up to the time of their stoppage. The closing of the works forced the majority of the experienced workmen to seek employment elsewhere.

In a brief history of the Church of Our Lady of Mount Carmel, the effect on the parish is noted: "The number of parishioners in 1874 was 1,743, but in 1876 this number had been reduced to 1,200." It further stated, ". . . the Rev. John O'Grady, D.D., came to Boonton on November 20, 1878, . . . the parish had now dwindled to 60 men, 66 women and 130 children." [245] The other churches of Boonton must have had proportionate losses in their congregations also.

Chapter VII

Attempts to Revive Operations

With the closing of the Boonton Ironworks in 1876, and the settlement of the joint interests in this large property, the estate of James Couper Lord came into the sole possession of the real estate, including mills, furnaces, mines and other property. William C. Lathrop continued to perform the duties of manager and overseer until his retirement, November, 1880.[246]

The deterioration of the properties and equipment during the years of idleness was considerable. The ravages of storms had taken their toll. A report of a hailstorm in 1879 stated that, "The hail-stones were as big as black walnuts and more than two thousand panes of glass were broken at the Boonton Ironworks."[247] A winter news item remarked that the machinery was covered with snow.

Nothing was found in the local paper in answer to the "Boonton Iron Works for Sale" advertisement for a period of eight months after its appearance. There were, however, some indications that the owners were making an effort to put the works in a more presentable condition. The first of several items had this to say:

> The owners of the furnaces in this place have discovered that the furnaces require greater repairs to put them in proper condition for use. It was thought that it would take but a few weeks to put them in condition for the fires; but then the workmen found them out of order to a much greater extent than was first supposed. The large engines and boilers were sadly in need of attention, and everything is now receiving the attention needed. It will take three or four weeks yet, probably more, to get the furnaces ready for use.[248]

Five weeks later the Christmas issue of the *Bulletin* headlined the following:

BOONTON IRON WORKS

One of the Blast Furnaces Lighted
The Beginning of Brighter Days for Boonton

As announced in last week's issue, one of the Furnaces which has been under repairs since October, was made ready for the match on Tuesday, the 23rd inst. From 15 to 20 cords of well seasoned hickory wood and a great many tons of coal were put in the Furnace before lighting, and the men were busy until noon of Tuesday. Shortly after one o'clock Mrs. J. Couper Lord and family and Mr. George Brown and two sons, accompanied by Messrs. W. G. Lathrop and Mr. H. C. Jenkins, entered the front arch of the Furnace, where quite a number of our citizens had gathered to witness the restarting of one of the Furnaces that had been out since March 1876. All being in readiness, Mr. Jenkins handed Miss Elsie B. Lord an Iron Cane finely polished for the occasion, the end being red hot. Miss Lord touched the shavings and immediately there was a high flame and in a few minutes the fire had passed into the great Furnace.

Some days will intervene before the first iron appears, but all will hail the good beginning with joy and hope the new year will bring with it much more for Boonton.

It is understood that the other Furnace will be at once prepared for work and will probably go in blast the latter part of January 1880.[249]

There were no comments by the editor or otherwise to be found in the local paper expressing how this display of pageantry was received. The thought of seeing the Ironworks in operation again probably outweighed any other thoughts that might have occurred at the time.

Two months later it was announced that Furnace No. 2 was ready to light.

In an article describing the operation of the furnaces an explanation was given of a change that was made: "Many have asked the question, 'Why is it the great light visible in former years is not seen at the blast furnaces in this place now?' The reason is, the burning gas which was formerly allowed to escape at the top of the furnaces is now thrown downward by caps, and utilized to assist in heating the blast, etc. At furnace No. 1 the burning gas is carried 40 feet downward. It is estimated that at least one ton of coal is thus saved to every ton of pig iron made." The pipe used to carry the burning gas downwards is appropriately named the "down-coiner."

The furnaces were in blast about three months when it was reported that in obedience to orders received from the New York office, the process of blowing out Furnace No. 2 was to take place. It was also said there were over three thousand ton of pig iron piled up at the furnace.[250]

Again it was reported that the force of workmen was considerably reduced at the Boonton Ironworks and those laid off had found work elsewhere.

In September 1880, it was announced that, "Mr. Tooke Straker is the new manager for the blast furnaces in Boonton. He will take the place of Mr. Henry Jenkins who will go into other business." [251]

Henry C. Jenkins had charge of the blast furnace operation since 1864, when he followed his father, George Jenkins, who had passed away early that year. George Jenkins had been in charge of the furnace since 1848, when the charcoal furnace was replaced with an anthracite-fired furnace. The change of furnaces was made by Samuel Thomas of Catasauqua, Pa. [252] He was the son of David Thomas who was affectionately styled the "Father of the American Anthracite-Iron Industry." [253]

In reference to Tooke Straker, who replaced Henry Jenkins, he was found to be in the employ of Joseph Wharton. It is believed that the Executors of the Lord Estate in their efforts to induce Joseph Wharton to purchase or lease the Boonton Works, agreed to have Tooke Straker in supervision of the operation of their furnaces. His knowledge and experience in the unproved processes of the industry probably brought about the change. Also, it gave Joseph Wharton a first-hand view of the situation and conditions as they existed at the Boonton Works.

Joseph Wharton

It would be difficult to enumerate and describe all of the business concerns that came to Boonton and attempted to establish themselves in the "hollow." The greatest effort was put forth by Joseph Wharton, of Philadelphia, Pa. It was apparent that the agents for the Boonton Works were in contact with Mr. Wharton at the time of the rebuilding and starting of the blast furnaces in the years 1879-80. The following news item is a fair introduction of Joseph Wharton and his intentions.

BOONTON IRON WORKS!

To be Started at Once.
Good News for Boonton.

Part of the Boonton Iron Works have been leased by Joseph Wharton, of Philadelphia, and will be started at once under the superintendence of Tooke Straker. Six of the puddling furnaces will be used at first, and the number will soon be increased to ten. The puddled iron will be made into muck and merchant bar, a large quantity of pig iron having been purchased, and will be in Boonton in a few days. The furnaces are being put into proper repair, and in the course of two or three weeks, the blaze will be seen issuing from them. Employment will be given about 150 hands.

We have no doubt that starting part of the works will lead to a complete restoration of business in all departments of the works, and we would not be surprised to hear the noise of the nail machines in a few months.

Mr. Wharton, the Lessee, is a wealthy and active gentleman, residing in Philadelphia, and is interested in the business of several large iron establishments. He is one of the principal owners of the Bethlehem iron works, and owns mills in other places.

He is the exclusive proprietor of the nickel works in this country, having a large establishment in Camden, in this State.

Mr. Wharton's reputation as one of the most successful business men in the United States is widespread. He is well known in Europe and is considered an authority in matters pertaining to the iron trade. He is a staunch advocate of high tariff frequently contributing leading articles on this important subject. We are glad that he has become interested in Boonton. Here is a grand field for the display of his powers, and we extend him in the name of all the citizens of the place a most cordial and hearty welcome.

A brighter day is dawning for Boonton. With such a gentleman as Joseph Wharton interested in the works here there can be no failure, if the people of the place will do their part to aid him in making the revival of our prostrated industry permanent.

Mr. Straker will exert all his energies in the matter, and will leave no stone unturned that will be for the interests of the works and the town in which they are located.[254]

However, Joseph Wharton's operation of the Boonton Works was of short duration. The foregoing announcement heralding his coming to Boonton was in August, 1881. The last item suggesting any connection with the Boonton Works was in March, 1883, which stated that "The nail mill project under consideration by Joseph Wharton is definitely abandoned. The other operations will close in the course of two months." [255]

Two other news briefs were found in 1883, one reporting Joseph Wharton's intention to build a rolling mill at Port Oram,[256] and the other noting the removal of 1,700 tons of pig iron from Boonton to his furnace at Port Gram.[257]

Mr. Wharton could not be criticized for his actions or preference in this matter. The furnace at Port Gram was much larger than either of the furnaces at Boonton, its capacity being 150,000 tons yearly.[258] The combined output of the two Boonton furnaces was 20,000 tons for the same period.[259]

The renaming of Port Gram to Wharton was effected by a special Act of the New Jersey Legislature on March 27, 1902. The new name was chosen to honor Joseph Wharton, industrialist and philanthropist, for his contribution to the growth and economy of that place.

Gen. John S. Schultze

The first mention of Gen. John S. Schultze in connection with the Boonton Works was in a news brief wherein Gen. Schultze was referred to as the superintendent of the Boonton Ironworks.[260] This was one week following the announcement of William Gerard Lathrop's retirement as Agent of the Boonton Ironworks.

Although Gen. Schultze was new to the citizens of Boonton, he was acquainted with the owners of the Works and their associates. In the report of the lighting of the blast furnace in December 1879, a Mr. George Brown and two sons were among those present. It was later said that during the Civil War Gen. Schultze saved the life of a wounded comrade officer, a connection, if not one of the brothers of Brown Bros., bankers in New York City. After the War, Gen. Schultze entered the employ of Brown Bros., in their extensive holdings. It was also said he was made president of one of the railroads in which the Brown Bros. had an interest.[261] The records show that Gen. Schultze was appointed Major and Asst. Adjutant General, Pennsylvania Volunteers, June 23, 1863, and that he was honorably discharged, November 22, 1865.[262]

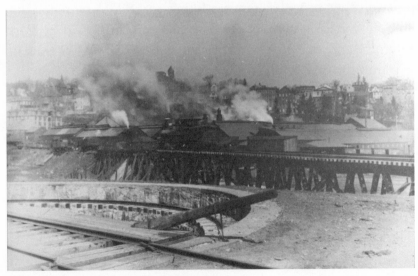

Boonton Ironworks. Trestle and railroad turntable.

Gen. Schultze lived in the manager's house formerly occupied by William G. Lathrop on Cornelia Street, about where the Elks Club is presently located, the grounds extending to Main Street. He purchased the house and the grounds from the Lord Estate in 1887.[263] During his years in the employ of the Lord Estate Gen. Schultze acted in the capacity of Agent rather than Superintendent, leasing the buildings and facilities to the various companies that sought to operate here. He also was a director and later vice-president of the Boonton National Bank.[264]

Gen. John S. Schultze died Easter Monday, April 8, 1912.[265]

The several attempts to revive the operation of the blast furnaces were without favorable results. In 1892 it was reported that the blast furnaces were about dismantled. The boilers, one blowing engine and a few other effects were all that was left to denote their former usefulness. The iron, etc., was being turned into profit. It was understood that all the cut stone that comprised the foundations and walls of the two blast furnaces would be torn down and shipped away.[266]

Demolishing part of the building on the upper nail factory site was begun.[267]

The large overshot waterwheel that was in use to run what was called the upper nail factory would be torn apart to make room for the new electric light plant flumes. They would enter the overflow above it, giving about fifty feet fall for the new turbine wheels.[268]

The period from 1885 to 1915 saw various companies start business in the buildings that comprised the old Boonton Ironworks. Almost all of those starting within this thirty-year period ended their operations for the same reason, Fire. The majority of these companies can be located on the Robinson Map of Boonton, N.J., 1900.

An attempt to revive the manufacture of nails was made in 1885, when Gen. Schultze made an agreement with three of our townsmen, Oscar Patterson, George Anthony and

William Grubb.[269] The lower nail factory was leased by these men and it was their intention to start with comparatively few machines. It was necessary to teach new help in the operation of the nail machines, for most of the former operators had moved away and were working at the trade elsewhere.

The Boonton nailworks continued with a moderate degree of success for about five years, but it was quite impossible to compete with the improved methods. No further reports were found referring to this operation until 1892, when it was stated that "Of about 200 nail machines that were kept in operation at one time, there are none left; they having all been disposed of." [270]

The New York Agricultural Works leased the Foundry in 1886, and made castings for agricultural machines. Later the Company used part of the old storehouse for machining parts and assembly.[271] The Foundry was a total loss by fire in 1915.[272]

The Lincoln Ironworks, often called the Bridleworks, came to Boonton in 1889.[273] The term "bridle" was given to a piece of heavy bar stock that was heated and shaped to hang over a girder and support the heavy beams in building construction. Anchor iron and architectural rivets were also manufactured here. The buildings of this Company adjoined the Boonton Iron & Steel Company's operation. The Lincoln Ironworks suffered total loss by fire, October 15, 1906.[274]

The W. C. Boone & Company and the Interchangeable Tool Company came to Boonton in 1890.[275] The W. C. Boone & Company stamped out pliers, nippers, metal shears, etc. The Interchangeable Tool Company did the necessary machine work to finish the products made here. The Interchangeable Tool Company moved from Boonton in September, 1893. The Standard Drop Forge Company is so named on the Robinson Map of Boonton, 1900, and the date of its termination could not be found.

The A. E. Norton Steel Company came to Boonton after 1905. The primary function of this company was the preparation of steel girders and associated products for construction and industrial purposes. The large girders and steel plates were shipped to Boonton and here they were cut and prepared for construction elsewhere. Several derricks and a traveling crane that encompassed the entire plant were used to move the large beams and assembled sections. The noise emanating from this works brought protestations from some of the citizens. A fire resulting in a total loss occurred in December, 1909,[276] and shortly thereafter the Norton Company moved to Jersey City where it became part of the Ryerson Steel Company of that place.

The Westinghouse Storage Battery Company came to Boonton about 1905 and was located in the large five-story masonry structure that was built by the Boonton Ironworks as a storehouse in 1867. Here large quantities of nails were stored in reserve to meet the demand of that period. The entire building was gutted by fire, February 6, 1910. The fire had gained great headway when detected at 6:30 that morning. When at its peak it was a spectacular sight because of the variety of brilliant colors of the flames. It was said the materials and chemicals used in the plant caused this display. By six o'clock in the evening all that was left was the bare walls and a mass of smoking ruin; bent girders, machinery, all heaped on the ground floor.[277]

Early Fire Protection

All of the fires in Boonton, until 1915, were fought with hand-drawn and hand-operated hose reels, pumping engines and bucket brigades. The Town of Boonton did not have an organized Fire Department until July 30, 1891. In Dr. John Grimes' first little newspaper, *The Monthly Advertiser*, mention is made of the Boonton Fire Company attending a Temperance Meeting at the Free Church.[278] This company was made up of men at the mills, and no mention was made of any protection for the rest of the community. Also, on February 2, 1881, this item appeared in *The Boonton Weekly Bulletin*:

A Fire Company's Relic—Fifty or sixty years ago Passaic Company No. 1 of Paterson, had a small hand engine. In the course of time it passed into the possession of the Boonton Iron Company, and has now been bought back by its original owners in Paterson for $25, to be preserved as a relic to be contrasted with their fine modern steamer.

In researching the history of the Boonton Fire Department, it was established that the little hand pumper was put in service in Paterson in 1821. It was brought to Boonton in 1835 and returned to Paterson in 1881.

A small engine built by Simeon VanDyne was used at the United States Hotel fire on August 20, 1892.[279] The following year Simeon VanDyne built two hand-pumpers for the Boonton Fire Department. These hand-pumpers were in service until a steam fire engine and two motor-driven chemical and hose engines were purchased in 1915.

One fire in particular is retained in the writer's mind probably because this was the last time the mill bell was heard to ring. It is used as an epilogue to this history.

Epilogue

The Ironworks in Boonton had a large bell in the cupola above the entrance to the Works, and its normal function was to tell the men when to start and stop their labors in the mill. Morning, noon and night the bell would be rung, tolling out its message for all to hear.

It was also used as an alarm signal for fires, accidents, etc., and if the bell sounded at a time other than usual, the cry of "There goes the mill bell" would send the townspeople scurrying to the mill to find out the cause of the excitement.

The last time the mill bell was heard to ring was at a fire in the Ironworks, October 15, 1906. It rang the alarm and it was kept ringing during the fire, until the men were driven from their post. The women, whose men labored in the mill, were standing along the railing in front of the author's home on Plane Street, watching the vain efforts to save the mill. Finally, when the supports were weakened by the flames, the mill bell toppled to the ground. The women wept.

1906 Fire, Boonton Ironworks.

In Retrospect. Falls at Boonton.

154

In Retrospect

The smoke and the din of the mills have long since left the valley. The glow of the furnaces lighting the sky at night, the forms of the men silhouetted against the open doors of the puddling furnaces, the spray of sparks as the "blooms" were put in the squeezers, shaping them to enter the rolls, the bright light of the white-hot bars passing through the rolls. The Clank! Clank! of the giant alligator shears, the iron bars being dropped into the cars, and the sharp exhaust of the drill engine in vehement protest to the load that was causing its wheels to spin.

The baleful sound of the boatman's horn calling the lock-tender or the plane-car, the huck-li-buck sound of the wire rope couplings as they passed over the pulleys that guided the wire-rope pulling the plane-car.

And then, on Sunday, when the Works were all quiet, the silence broken only by the sounds of the river tumbling over the falls and through the gorge, all part of the scene that happened here, long ago.

Appendix

Boonton's Little Cannon

The restoration of the Boonton Cannon brought about an interesting bit of research, for the process of removing the barrel from the carriage allowed a thorough examination of the various parts of the cannon. Cannon barrels usually have distinguishing marks or symbols which were carefully looked for, but none were found. However, an examination of the bore with a flashlight revealed a gas-pocket or off-center enlargement of the breech cavity at the bottom of the bore. This defect at once called to mind a published letter from Joseph Hoff, who under Lord Sterling was manager of the Adventure Furnace at Hibernia. The letter was dated August 3rd, 1776. It stated that—"Last night we made a trial at casting one of the guns, but unfortunately for us we brought the furnace too low and it missed in the breech. All the rest was sound and good." Could it be possible that the reputed Boonton 1860 cannon was actually a surviving Revolutionary War cannon cast at Hibernia in 1776?

I related my findings and thoughts to my good friend, Harold W. Schroeder, a very capable historian who also had a metallurgical background. To my question, "Is there any way of testing the iron of the cannon to determine the period of its casting?" the answer was, "Yes." Mr. Schroeder explained that the Adventure Furnace at Hibernia was built in 1765, made nothing but cast iron, using cold blast with charcoal for fuel, and sold pig iron for refining by neighboring forges. The first Boonton furnace, built in 1833, was also a cold blast charcoal furnace. It was replaced in 1848 with a larger hot blast furnace which used anthracite coal, brought in on the Morris Canal, which also brought local ores including ore from Hibernia. The pig iron made at this Boonton furnace was then refined in puddling furnaces, rolled into plates, and made into cut nails.

It was decided to compare chemistries—a sample taken from the Boonton cannon, and a sample positively identified as the

Hibernia iron of 1776. Then the search began for authentic Hibernia iron. Washington's Headquarters Museum at Morristown had a genuine Hibernia pig with the name cast on it. The Montgomery County Historical Society had a Hibernia cast iron stove plate in their museum at Fort Johnson, New York. The New Jersey Historical Society had a Hibernia stove plate in their museum at Newark, N.J. None of the three were willing to risk damage to their museum exhibits by allowing borings or samples to be taken from the underside of the pieces. *The Newark News* helped with a news article that brought a piece of iron taken from the brook below the site of the old furnace at Hibernia. This piece, found by Fred F. Mitchko of Boonton Township, gave us the first sample, although it did not have any identifying marks.

The prospect of getting an authenticated piece of Hibernia iron seemed hopeless, but several weeks later Mr. Schroeder called and told me of a piece of pig, dated 1770, that was found on the site of Old Middle Forge, that was part of the Charlotteburg works. I questioned the use of a sample taken from this 1770 pig, in the belief that it was made from iron ore mined at Charlotteburg. Mr. Schroeder informed me that the Charlotteburg mine was not opened until the following year, and the iron ore used in 1770 was carted to the Charlotteburg furnace from Hibernia.

The archeological group of the North Jersey Highlands Historical Society had been working the Middle Forge site, and among the artifacts uncovered was a piece of pig iron with the year 1770 cast on its surface. Edward Lenik, known for his contributions published in the *Proceedings of the New Jersey Historical Society*, and whose slide lectures have been enjoyed by many, had uncovered this piece of pig. Upon inquiry it was learned that James Norman, another member of the group, had the piece at his home in Newfoundland, N.J. I visited Mr. Norman and told him of the problem encountered in my quest for an authenticated piece of Hibernia Iron cast in the manner used in the period of the Revolution. Without hesitation he very generously suggested that I cut a small portion from the back of the 1770 piece of pig iron.

157

The net result in acquiring this sample was—having failed to get samples of authenticated iron of the Revolutionary period from the Hibernia furnace, we succeeded in getting an authentic sample of cold blast charcoal furnace pig, made in the Charlotteburg furnace instead of the Hibernia furnace, being duplicate furnaces using duplicate practices and using the same Hibernia ore, ensured by there being no other source of iron nearby that could have been available to these furnaces at that time.

Accordingly, Mr. Schroeder sent our samples to the laboratory of one of the larger steel companies where old friends of his performed the chemical analysis. The samples analyzed were: (1) a sample of the Charlotteburg pig; (2) a sample cut from the end of the broken trunnion of the Boonton Little Cannon; and (3) a piece from the sample found in the brook below the site of the Adventure Furnace at Hibernia.

Summarizing the laboratory report:

1. Sample No. 1 is authentic Hibernia ore by definition, cast into pig iron dated 1770 at the Charlotteburg furnace; analyzed to contain Carbon 3.25%.

2. Sample No. 3 is also from Hibernia ore, cast into pig iron plate at the Hibernia furnace; Carbon 3.33%.

3. Because of its carbon content of 0.022%, Sample No. 2 could not have been cast at Hibernia from the furnace direct, although the other non-oxidizable elements show show that it came from Hibernia ore.

4. In that period, Carbon 0.022% could only have been cast from remelted refinery forge iron.

5. Boonton furnace sometimes used Hibernia ore, its pig iron was decarburized in its own refinery forges and rolled into nail plate for its own cut nail manufacture; and in 1857 it had built a foundry with a capacity of 400 tons per year, to supply the castings needed throughout the mills.

6. "Legend tells us that the barrel was made of Boonton nails melted down for that purpose." Apparently this was not as questionable as it seemed and we do not know of any other nearby foundry which could have cast the cannon.

Notes

Chapter 1

1. E. N. Hartley, *Ironworks on the Saugus*, Norman: University of Oklahoma Press, 1957, pp. 4, 5, 153.

2. *Documents Relating to the Colonial History of the State of New Jersey*, edited by William A. Whitehead, Vol. VII, 1746-1751, p. 558. (New Jersey Archives, 1st series, Vol. VII).

3. Holograph letter, Samuel Ogden to Robert Morris, 4 February, 1778, (collections of Historical Society of Pennsylvania) mentions furnishing large quantities of camp kettles, axes, nails, etc.; letter, T. Pickering, QMC, to Capt. Walker, Aidede-Camp, Newburgh, March 22, 1783 (Library of Congress) mentions orders for 1,800 camp kettles from Samuel Ogden; James Abeel's letter book (EN169 N.J. Historical Society), p. 86, a "number of Iron Cups" received from Mr. Ogden, p. 114, Col. Ogden agrees to furnish 6,000 pairs of horseshoes & deliver same to DQM Gen. James Abeel; *Minutes of the Council of Safety of the State of New Jersey*, 1778, Jersey City, 1872, p. 214: "Agreed that Col. Hathaway received from Mr. Ogden, at Boonton, the 20,000 flints sent or to be sent into this State, by Mr. Archibald Mercer, from Boston . . . " dated March 17, 1778.

4. *History of Morris County, New Jersey*, W. W. Munsell & Co., New York, 1882 (hereafter, "Munsell"), pp. 48-56.

5. *Ibid.*, p. 51.

6. "Copy of Journal of – – – Reading, April 17th to June 10th, 1715," Proc. N.J. Hist. Soc., Vol. X, Third Series, 1915.

7. James Alexander Records, p. 148 (from notes of Philip H. Wadell Smith).

8. Samuel Harris' Account Book, p. 67 (NJHS): Burnett Papers 1856 (NJHS): Conger's Monumental Inscriptions, p. 356 (NJHS).

9. W. O. Wheeler and E. D. Halsey, *Inscriptions on Tombstones and Monuments in the Grave Yards at Whippany and Hanover, Morris County, N.J.*, p. 1.

10. Annette C. Ball, *History of the Parsippany, New Jersey Presbyterian Church* (prepared for the Centennial Celebration, June 17-20, 1928), p. 17.

11. Morris County Deeds, Book C, p. 80, May 1, 1797. Conveyance of land formerly property of Obadiah Baldwin, Sr., deceased.

12. Records of Proprietors of East Jersey, Book S-4, p. 200.

13. Morris County Roads, Book A, No. 8, March 31, 1761.

14. Ambrose E. Vanderpoel (Editor), *Personal Memoirs of Edwin A. Ely*, Charles Francis Press, New York, 1926, pp. 64-67, for an account of William Kelly.

15. New Jersey Archives, 1st Series, Vol. IX, pp. 234, 306.

16. *Ibid.*, Vol. XXVII, p. 521, advertisement of July 15, 1771.

17. *Ibid.*, Vol. XXVIII, pp. 372-3, advertisement of Dec. 28, 1772.

18. Deeds, Book B-3, pp. 324-328, State Library, Trenton, N.J.

19. Deeds, Book C-3, p. 315, State Library. On July 1, 1773, Samuel Ogden bought 341 acres of land in vicinity of Old Boonton from the heirs of Thomas Stevenson.

20. Morris County Ancient Deeds, Book 1, p. 191. Quit-claim deed from David Ogden to John Ball, April 21, 1774, refers to adjacent land Samuel Ogden purchased from David Ogden; David Ogden's will, Book A, p. 439, Jamaica, Long Island, mentions the Boonton estate which Samuel bought from his father in or about the year 1770.

21. Isaac S. Lyon, *Historical Discourse on Boonton*, Newark, 1873, p. 12.

22. *Ibid.*, p. 13 (hereafter, "Lyon").

23. Same as Note 16.

24. Munsell, p. 280.

25. Advertisement in *New York Packet* of Sept. 27, 1781.

26. New Jersey Archives, 1st series, Vol. VII, pp. 554-5, 558-9.

27. *Ibid.*, Vol. X, p. 372.

28. New Jersey Archives, 1st series, Vol. XVIII, p. 172.

29. *Ibid.*, p. 359.

30. New Jersey Archives, 1st series, Vol. XXIX, p. 425.

31. *Ibid.*, Vol. XXXI, p. 54.

32. *Penna. Chron. & Universal Advertiser*, Mar. 27, 1769 (Ely coil., NJHS): Von Beverhoudt Letterbook, Oct. 7, 1779 (Morristown Nat'l Historical Park Library); Evelyn M. Acomb (ed. & translator), *The Revolutionary Journal of Baron Ludwig von Closen 1780-1783*, University of North Carolina Press, Chapel Hill, 1958, p. 113; Lyon, p. 6; Munsell, p. 218.

33. Proc. NJHS, new series, Vol. XI, No. 4, pp. 458-467, for Ogden Loyalists.

34. David Ogden's will (see note 20) in re Abraham Ogden; Munsell, p. 56, for Samuel Ogden's purchases.

35. *Minutes of the Council of Safety of the State of New Jersey*, 1777-8, p. 69, 73.

36. Ambrose Ely Vanderpoel, *History of Chatham, New Jersey*, republished by Chatham Historical Society, 1959, pp. 171-2.

37. Letter, Maxwell to Washington, Feb. 17, 1777 (Library of Congress).

38. Committee of Safety, *op. cit.*, p. 274.

39. *Dictionary of American Biography* (DAB), Vol. XIII, 1943, pp. 642-3.

40. John C. Fitzpatrick (Ed.), *Writings of George Washington*, Vol. 26, Jan. 19, 1783, Government Printing Office, Washington, D.C.

41. Same as Note 3.

42. Albert H. Heusser, *The Forgotten General, Robert Erskine, F.R.S.*, Benjamin Franklin Press, Paterson, N.J., 1928, p. 115; James M. Ransom, *Vanishing Ironworks of the Ramapos*, Rutgers University Press, New Brunswick, N.J., 1966, p. 40.

43. Records of the State of New Jersey, Department of Defense, as certified Oct. 19, 1961.

44. Tax Ratables for County of Morris for the year 1778 (State Library, Trenton, N.J.; microfilms of same, Morris County Historical Society).

45. Fitzpatrick, *op. cit.*, Vol. 8, p. 375; *Ibid.*, Vol. 23, p. 534.

46. Erskine's Map No. 90-B, collections of New York Historical Society.

47. *Boonton Times-Bulletin*, Oct. 28, 1941, shows picture of Faesch Mansion and describes its position with respect to bridge and roads existing about 1898.

48. Morris County Mortgages, Book F, p. 232, gives position of foot-bridge with respect to forge and slitting mill lot.

49. Deed cited in Note 19 gives position of Stagg's house with respect to Ogden's house, i.e., by calculation to be about 290 feet east of Ogden's.

50. Morris County Roads, Book A, pp. 144-5, Aug. 31, 1786.

51. Map of Reservoir, showing roads, property lines and contours, made for Jersey City Water Supply Co. in 1903, retraced 1915 (Map in possession of Boonton Historical Society).

52. Morris County Deeds, Book A, p. 281, for Compson; Morris County Mortgages, Book B, p. 316, for Davies.

53. Samuel Ogden, Thomas Compson and Thomas Davies seem to have been affiliated with the Parsippany Presbyterian Church as late as 1773, *cf.* Ball, *op. cit.*, reference Note 10.

54. Note Book of Frances Willis (Mrs. B. F. Howell), p. 7 (collections of Princeton University Library).

55. Map of Morris County, New Jersey, from Surveys of J. Lightfoot and Samuel Geil, published by J. B. Shields, Morristown, 1853 (republished 1964, by Morris County Tercentenary Committee).

56. Records, Reformed Church of Montville, N.J., Vol. I; Journals of the Diocese of New Jersey, 1808, report of the Rev. Joseph Willard.

57. Lyon, p. 15.

58. New Jersey Archives, 1st series, Vol. XXXXI, will of Samuel Ogden, proved Jan. 23, 1813, pp. 279-280; also DAB for David B. Ogden.

59. Lyon, p. 14; Morris County Deeds, Book A, p. 21-23, May 1, 1784, gives Samuel Ogden's place of residence as New York, and occupation as merchant.

60. Munsell, pp. 53-4; *Biographical and Genealogical History of Morris County, New Jersey*, Lewis Publishing Company, 1899 (hereafter,

"Lewis, 1899"), pp. 258-9; Faesch Papers (part of John Jacob
Faesch collection owned by Town of Boonton).

61. Faesch Papers, manuscript sheet of vital records.
62. New Jersey Archives, 1st series, Vol. XXV, pp. 160-3.
63. Lewis, 1899, pp. 258-9.
64. Munsell, p. 53.
65. Faesch Papers, vital records.
66. Ransom, *op. cit.*, pp. 110-115; Munsell, pp. 54-55; Letter Books
of Joseph and Charles Hoff (Morristown Nat'l Historical Park
Library).
67. Faesch Papers, vital records.
68. Proc. NJHS, Vol. 62, No. 1, Whole No. 236, Jan. 1944, p. 41,
"Diary of Joseph Lewis."
69. Faesch Papers, vital records.
70. Munsell, p. 56.
71. *Cazenove Journal 1794*, ed. ,by Raynor Wickersham Kelsey. The
Pennsylvania History Press, 1922.
72. *Under Their Vine and Fig Tree*, Julian Ursyn Niemcewicz, translated
and edited with an Introduction by Metchie J. E. Budka.
Vol. XIV of Collections of N.J. Historical Society, 1965,
pp. 27-8, 227-8.
73. Memorandum of Thomas C. Willis to Isaac S. Lyon, Sept. 1,
1859, *Boonton Times-Bulletin*, Feb. 21, 1941; Lyon, p. 15.
74. Faesch Papers, vital records; Combined Register, First
Presbyterian Church of Morristown, N.J., p. 69.
75. Morris County Deeds, Book K, p. 430; Morris County Mortgages,
Book F, p. 232 (purchase mortgage).
76. Same as Note 74.
77. Morris County Marriages, Book A, p. 121; Faesch Papers, vital
records.
78. Morris County Deeds, Book L-2, p. 340.
79. Munsell, p. 281.
80. *Ibid.*, p. 281.
81. Morris County Deeds, Book P-2, p. 598.
82. DeCamp Papers (Morris County Historical Society), account of
building materials sold to William Scott.
83. *A Gazetteer of the State of New Jersey*, by Thomas Cordon, Trenton,
1834, pp. 23-26, an account of Morris Canal.
84. Atlas of Morris Canal, County Clerk's Office, Morristown, N.J.
85. Lyon, p. 15.
86. Same as Note 85.
87. Morris County Deeds, Book U-3, p. 331.
88. Munsell, p. 281.
89. Morris County Deeds, Book X-3, p. 326; Mortgages, Book 5,

p. 283; Deeds, Book D-9, p. 463 (Sheriff's deed to Wm. A. Righter, May 22, 1875).

90. Morris County Deeds, Book M-9, p. 1 (Wm. A. Righter and wife to Philip Wootton); Deeds, Book L-10, p. 256 (Jas. Holmes and wife, Wm. C. Lathrop and wife, and Philip Wootton and wife to Maurice Fitz Gibbon and Arthur J. Messer).

91. *Boonton Weekly Bulletin*, issues of 5/20/1880, 6/2/'81, 8/3/'83, 4/14/'87, 1/26/'88, 7/2/'91 and 9/17/'91 recount construction of paper mill, Fitz Gibbon sojourn at Polly Board house, and refurbishing of historic mansion.

92. Morris County Deeds, Book U-17, p. 408.

Chapter 2

93. Same as Note 83.

94. *Historical Collections of the State of New Jersey*, John W. Barber and Henry Howe, New York, 1844, pp. 231-401.

95. Morris County Deeds, Book P-2, p. 598.

96. Morris County Roads, Book C, p. 78, also Book C, p. 135.

97. Munsell, p. 179.

98. Morris County Deeds, Book X-2, p. 489 (William Scott and wife to David W. Wetmore, August 24, 1829).

99. Morris County Deeds, Book C-3, p. 258 (David Wetmore and wife to New Jersey Iron Co., November 30, 1830).

100. Munsell, p. 179.

101. "Pioneer Days in Boonton, N.J.," Cora E. Hammond, Proceedings NJHS, Vol. VIII, No. 4, October 1923, pp. 287-289.

102. *Seventy-fifth Anniversary of the First Presbyterian Church, Boonton, N.J.*, Oct. 27, 1907. Booklet contains "History of the Sunday School" by Henry C. Jenkins, p. 36.

103. *Boonton Weekly Bulletin*, Samuel L. Garrison, Editor, September 17, 1874. "First Congregational Society of Boonton, N.J." incorporated April 19, 1841. John Grimes, George Esten, James S. Norris and Daniel C. Norris elected trustees and incorporators.

104. Munsell, p. 179.

105. *Manual for the Members of the First Presbyterian Church of Boonton Falls, N.J. 1850.*" (This Manual was found by the author in the attic of his home in 1923. Later, in 1962, the Manual was presented to Miriam Carter Conn, who was Clerk of the Session of the Church at the time.)

106. Booklet, *Golden Jubilee 1847-1897, Church of Our Lady of Mount Carmel*. (annotations by Helen Dunn).

107. Letter, Rev. D. C. Castet to A. B. Cobb. (Original letter in collections of author presented to Helen Dunn, historian of Our Lady of Mt. Carmel Church, 1974).

108. Munsell, pp. 183-185.
109. Same as Note 106.
110. Munsell, pp. 180-181.
111. Map, "Survey of Boonton New Jersey," by James E. Serrell, Chief Engineer, 1848. Burnett & Serrell & Co., New York. (Copy of Letter of acceptance and agreement, Peter C. Wendt, Jr., to Homer W. Dixon).
112. Lewis, 1899, Vol. I, pp. 16-22.
113. Munsell, p. 180.
114. Munsell, p. 181.
115. Munsell, p. 185.
116. *The Jerseyman*, a weekly newspaper published in Morristown, N.J., edition of Oct. 13, 1860 (hereafter, *The Jerseyman*).
117. Lyon, p. 54.
118. Same as Note 117.
119. Interview with Wm. Carson, Jr., now deceased, who was a grandson of John Carson, Sr.
120. Lyon, p. 31.
121. Lewis, 1899, Vol. II, p. 491.
122. *A History of Morris County, New Jersey*, Lewis Historical Publishing Co., New York and Chicago, 1914. Vol. II, pp. 190-191 (hereafter, "Lewis, 1914").
123. Lewis, 1914, Vol. I, pp. 105-106.
124. Dr. John Grimes' "Day Book," containing a record of patients' names and treatment given, was presented to the New Jersey Highlands Historical Society by Norman Grimes, formerly of Parsippany. This book recorded the years of Dr. Grimes' practice prior to his coming to Boonton in 1833.
125. Lewis, 1914, Vol. I, pp. 115-116.
126. *The Journal of John Woolman* with an introduction by John C. Whittier, Boston: James R. Osgood & Co., 1871, pp. 80-81.
127. *The American Conflict: A History of the Great Rebellion in the United States of America*, 1860-1865, by Horace Greeley, Published by O. D. Case & Co., Vol. I, p. 119 (hereafter, *The American Conflict*).
128. Munsell, pp. 53-54.
129. *Dorothy Delafield*, Mary Harriott Norris, New York: Hunt & Eaton; Cincinnati: Cranston & Howe, 1889, pp. 9-10.
130. *The American Conflict*, Vol. 1, 123-124.
131. *New Jersey as a Colony and as a State*, Francis Bazley Lee, New York: The Publishing Society of New Jersey, 1903. Vol. IV, pp. 51-58 (hereafter, "Lee, 1903").
132. Charles F. Hopkins, manuscript describing the activities of the "Underground Railroad" from the personal reminiscences of Charles F. Hopkins.
133. *Boonton Weekly Bulletin*, Sept. 16, 1875. Obit. Dr. John Grimes.

134. Lee, 1903, pp. 65-67.
135. *The Jerseyman*, Sept. 8, 1860, Sept. 15, 1860.
136. *The Jerseyman*, Oct. 6, 1860.
137. *The Jerseyman*, Sept. 8, 1860, Sept. 15, 1860.
138. See appendix, Boonton's Little Cannon.

Chapter 3

139. *The Jerseyman*, April 12, 1861.
140. *The American Conflict*, Vol. I, pp. 453-454.
141. *The Jerseyman*, Sept. 6, 1862.
142. *The Jerseyman*, April 12, 1861. Reprint of article from the *Paterson Guardian*.
143. *The Jerseyman*, May 2, 1861.
144. Charles F. Hopkins, personal reminiscences, pp. 27-28, manuscript in collection of author.
145. *The Jerseyman*, July 20, 1861.
146. *The Jerseyman*, May 3, 1862.
147. *The Jerseyman*, Feb. 1, 1862.
148. Charles F. Hopkins, personal reminiscences, manuscript, pp. 27-28.
149. Medal of Honor Certificate, No. 201, issued under the provisions of the Act of Congress approved April 27, 1916, to Charles F. Hopkins.
150. *The Jerseyman*, July 12, 1862.
151. *The Jerseyman*, Aug. 2, 1862.
152. *The Jerseyman*, Sept. 6, 1862.
153. *The Jerseyman*, Sept. 6, 1862.
154. *The Jerseyman*, Sept. 13, 1862.
155. *The Jerseyman*, April 18, 1863.
156. *The Jerseyman*, April 18, 1863.
157. Munsell, p. 181.
158. *The Jerseyman*, May 2, 1863. Morris Canal and Banking Co., Statement of Finances.
159. Lyon, p. 54.
160. Shipping Book of Martin Shaw, 1866-1870. Collection of author.
161. *The Jerseyman*, May 2, 1863.
162. *The Jerseyman*, May 9, 1863.
163. This incident was related to the author in detail in separate interviews with R. Percy Ralston and John E. Myers.
164. *The Jerseyman*, July 9, 1863.
165. State of New Jersey, Department of Defense, Service Record of James Plant.
166. *The Jerseyman*, Aug. 1, 1863.
167. *The Jerseyman*, Dec. 12, 1863.
168. *The Jerseyman*, Jan. 23, 1864.
169. *The Jerseyman*, Jan. 30, 1864.
170. *The Jerseyman*, Feb. 6, 1864.

171. *The Jerseyman*, March 19, 1864.
172. *The Jerseyman*, April 16, 1864.
173. *The Jerseyman*, June 4, 1864.
174. John Hill Letter: Expressing thanks for gift of $170 for his efforts in filling quota with volunteers. Original letter in author's collection.
175. *The Jerseyman*, May 21, 1864.
176. *The Jerseyman*, May 21, 1864.
177. *The Jerseyman*, June 18, 1864.
178. *The Jerseyman*, Nov. 5, 1864.
179. *The Jerseyman*, Dec. 24, 1864.
180. *The Jerseyman*, July 23, 1864.
181. *The Jerseyman*, April 15, 1865.
182. *The Jerseyman*, April 15, 1865.
183. *The Jerseyman*, April 22, 1865.

Chapter 4

184. *The Jerseyman*, July 15, 1865.
185. See Note 220, infra.
186. *Boonton Weekly Bulletin*, Samuel L. Garrison, Editor and Publisher. Dec. 2, 1875 (hereafter, "*B.W.B.*").
187. *B.W.B.*, July 6, 1876.

Chapter 5

188. Lewis, 1899, Vol. II, p. 417.
189. *The Jerseyman*, Nov. 4, 1865.
190. *The Jerseyman*, Nov. 11, 1865.
191. *The Jerseyman*, April 14, 1866.
192. *The Jerseyman*, April 14, 1866.
193. *The Jerseyman*, Sept. 8, 1866.
194. *The Jerseyman*, Sept. 15, 1866.
195. *B.W.B.*, July 24, 1884.
196. *The Jerseyman*, Nov. 10, 1866.
197. *B.W.B.* (Supplement), July 31, 1884.
198. *B.W.B.* (Supplement), July 31, 1884.
199. Lewis, 1899, Vol. II, p. 418.
200. *B.W.B.*, July 24, 1884.
201. Lewis, 1899, Vol. II, p. 419.
202. *B.W.B.*, July 24, 1884.
203. *B.W.B.* (Supplement), July 31, 1884.
204. *B.W.B.*, May 28, 1885.
205. Lewis, 1899, Vol. II, pp. 676-677.
206. Map of Boonton, N.J., E. Robinson & Co., New York, N.Y., 1900.
207. Lewis, 1899, Vol. II, pp. 677-679.
208. *History of Schools in Morris County, N.J.*, by L. W. Thurber, 1876; Montville, Pequannock and Boonton, pp. 1-50, written by John L.

Kanouse. Original copy in Special Collections, Rutgers University, New Brunswick, N.J. (hereafter, *History of Schools, M.C.N.J.*).

209. *History of Schools*, M.C.N.J., pp. 4, 5, 10, 11, 23.
210. *History of Schools*, M.C.N.J., p. 25.
211. *History of Schools*, M.C.N.J., pp. 25-27.
212. *History of Schools*, M.C.N.J., pp. 27-28.
213. *The Jerseyman*, Aug. 18, 1853.
214. *History of Schools*, M.C.N.J., p. 29.
215. *History of Schools*, M.C.N.J., pp. 30-31.
216. *History of Schools*, M.C.N.J., p. 31.
217. Munsell, p. 286. "Atlas of Morris Co., New Jersey," F. W. Beers, New York, 1868, p. 28.
218. Munsell, p. 184.
219. Munsell, pp. 184-185.

Chapter 6

220. *Revised Ordinances of the Town of Boonton, New Jersey*, 1956. Edited by George Clark, Municipal Codes, Inc., Boonton, Preface, III.
221. *B.W.B.*, Aug. 28, 1873. (The loss reported at $60,000 appears to be low. See Munsell, p. 181, for inventory of Boonton ironworks.) *B.W.B.*, Sept. 4, 1873.
222. *B.W.B.*, Dec. 18, 1873.
223. *B.W.B.*, June 11, 1874. Compare Boonton maps in Beers' Atlas of M.C. 1868 and Robinson's Atlas of MC., 1887, for change of names on various lots in Boonton.
224. *B.W.B.*, July 6, 1876.
225. Munsell, p. 180.
226. *B.W.B.*, Sept. 16, 1875.
227. *B.W.B.*, Nov. 11, 1875.
228. *B.W.B.*, April 15, 1880.
229. *B.W.B.*, Aug. 12, 1880; *B.W.B.*, Nov. 4, 1880.
230. *B.W.B.*, June 2, 1881.
231. *B.W.B.*, June 9, 1881.
232. *B.W.B.*, Feb. 1, 1883.
233. *B.W.B.*, Nov. 17, 1887; *B.W.B.*, Aug. 30, 1888.
234. Letter to Mrs. Lord and copies of newspaper clippings, etc., relative to the meetings of the Boonton workingmen at Washington Hall in the collections of the Boonton Historical Society; also, see *B.W.B.*, Aug. 19, 1876; Aug. 26, 1876; Sept. 2, 1876, and Sept. 9, 1876.
235. *B.W.B.*, Jan. 4, 1877.
236. Miss Jessie Phillips interview, tape in collections of the author.
237. *B.W.B.*, May 9, 1878.
238. *B.W.B.*, Jan. 3, 1878.
239. *B.W.B.*, June 13, 1878.

240. *B.W.B.*, Feb. 6, 1879.
241. *B.W.B.*, March 6, 1879.
242. *B.W.B.*, March 13, 1879.
243. *B.W.B.*, May 15, 1879.
244. *B.W.B.*, March 13, 1879.
245. Same as Note 106.

Chapter 7

246. *B.W.B.*, Oct. 21, 1880.
247. *B.W.B.*, Sept. 11, 1880.
248. *B.W.B.*, Nov. 20, 1879.
249. *B.W.B.*, Dec. 25, 1879.
250. *B.W.B.*, May 27, 1880.
251. *B.W.B.*, Sept. 20, 1880.
252. Munsell, p. 180.
253. *Iron in All Ages*, Swank, 1884, p. 273.
254. *B.W.B.*, Aug. 4, 1881.
255. *B.W.B.*, March 15, 1883.
256. *B.W.B.*, April 12, 1883.
257. *B.W.B.*, Dec. 13, 1883.
258. Munsell, p. 60.
259. Munsell, p. 60.
260. *B.W.B.*, Oct. 28, 1880.
261. Interview, Miss Joy DeCamp—Alex. D. Fowler.
262. Department of Interior, Bureau of Pensions, Washington, D.C., June 6, 1911.
263. *B.W.B.*, March 3, 1887.
264. *B.W.B.*, Jan. 30, 1890.
265. *B.W.B.*, April 11, 1912.
266. *B.W.B.*, March 10, 1892.
267. *B.W.B.*, June 23, 1892.
268. *B.W.B.*, July 28, 1892.
269. *B.W.B.*, Dec. 17, 1885.
270. *B.W.B.*, March 10, 1892.
271. *B.W.B.*, Dec. 16, 1886.
272. Minute Book, Maxfield Hose Co., No. 1 Boonton Fire Department (hereafter, "Maxfield Minute Book").
273. *B.W.B.*, March 28, 1889.
274. Maxfield Minute Book.
275. *B.W.B.*, Aug. 14, 1890.
276. Maxfield Minute Book.
277. Maxfield Minute Book.
278. *The Monthly Advertiser*, Dr. John Grimes, Boonton, N.J. Sept. 30, 1843. Vol. 1, No. 3.
279. *B.W.B.*, Aug. 25, 1892.

INDEX

172

Gordon, Harry, 43
Grace Lord monument, 45
Great Boonton Tract, 5
Green, Archibald D., 137
Green, Robert, 103
Green Street, 42, 138
Green, William, 31, 42
Green, William, Jr., 39
Greenbank Road, Parsippany, 11
Grimes, Hulda Leonard (Mrs. Jonathan Casper), 50
Grimes, James, 57
Grimes, Doctor John, 48-53, 55-58, 70, 85, 116, 151; member of Union League, 78; officer of Anti-Slavery Society, 51
Grimes, Jonathan Casper, 50
Gristmill and forge at Powerville, 28
Gristmill, Old Boonton, 1, 7, 12, 18
"Grove, The," 98-99
Grubb, William, 138, 150
Grubb, Mrs. William, 138
Gunning, Reverend J. H., 106

Hailstorm, 1879, 143
Haley, Patrick, 89
Halseytown (Parsippany), 50
Hammond, Cora E., 31
Hammond, Thomas, and sons, Enoch and Thomas, 31
Hammonds, Mr. and Mrs. Samuel, 138
Hammonds, Mr. and Mrs. Thomas, 138
Hanover Township, 1, 3, 5, 10, 103, 119, 129; war tax in, 83
Harper's New Monthly Magazine, July, 1860, 21
Harrison Street, 125; School, 124-125
Hasenclever, Peter, 14
Heath, Hugh, 61

Heating furnaces, 43
Hegman, Johanetta Elizabeth. *See*: Faesch, Johanetta Elizabeth Hegman
Hibernia, 2, 22; blast furnace at, 16; mines, 1
Highland Avenue, 29
Hill, John, 42, 77, 86, 88-90, 107-116, 137; Civil War enlistments and volunteers, 66, 74-76, 85, 87; Congressman, 1867-1874, 107-108; elected to House of Assembly, 109-110; flag-raising speaker, 70; member of Lincoln and Hamlin Club, 59; member of Union League, 78; purse of money presented to, 87; Silk factory dedication, present at, 131; State Senator, 1874, 108; Sunday School leader, 112; Union League member, 78, with underground movement, 57
Hill, Mrs. John, 138
Historical Discourse on Boonton, 2, 51
Hoboken, 69
Hodgkins Building. *See*: Ball Building
Hodgkins, John, and children, Lavina and James, 31
Hodgkins, Mrs. John, and children, Betsy, Mary, Sarah and Thomas, 31
Hodgkins, Joseph, 138
Hoffman, Nicholas, 6, 8
Holland, John, 37
Holland Land Company, 15
"Hollow, The," 63, 146
Holman, James, 122
Holmes, James, 18, 37, 137
Homan, J. H., 102, 105
Home Guard, 61
Hopkins, Charles F., 57;